Mandala Coloring Book No. 9:
32 New Intricate Round Mandala Designs

by Alberta Hutchinson

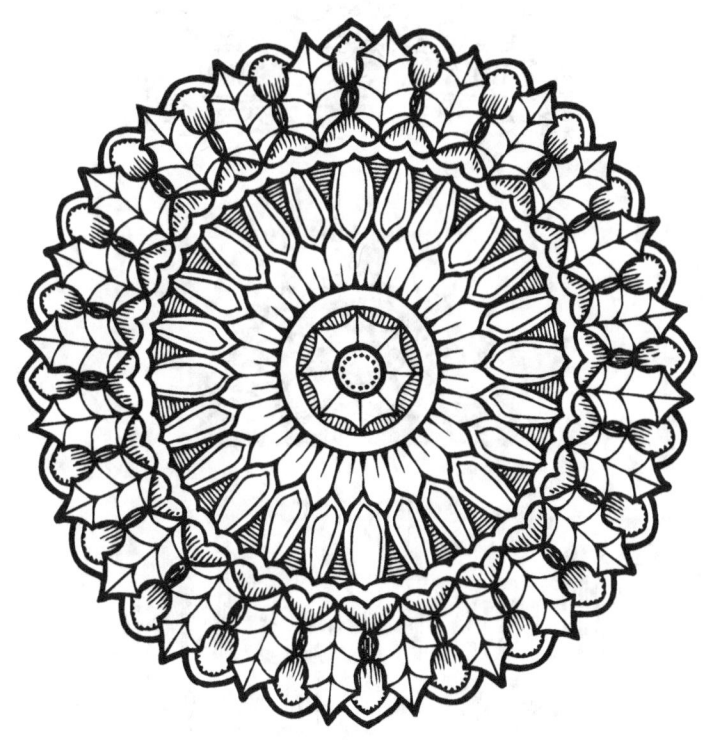

This coloring book is part of the
Hutchinson Mandala Coloring Book Collection

A book list of the Hutchinson Collection
appears in the back of this book.

Illume Writers & Artists

Mandala Coloring Book No. 9: 32 New Intricate Round Mandala Designs,
Copyright © 2016 by Alberta L. Hutchinson
All rights reserved

ISBN: 978-1517164089

Hutchinson Mandala Coloring Book Collection

Series:

Published by:

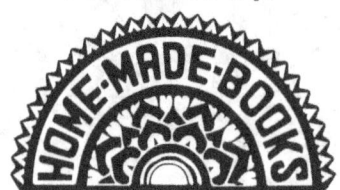

An Imprint of

Illume Writers & Artists
PO Box 86, Gilbertsville, NY 13776

Printed in the United States of America

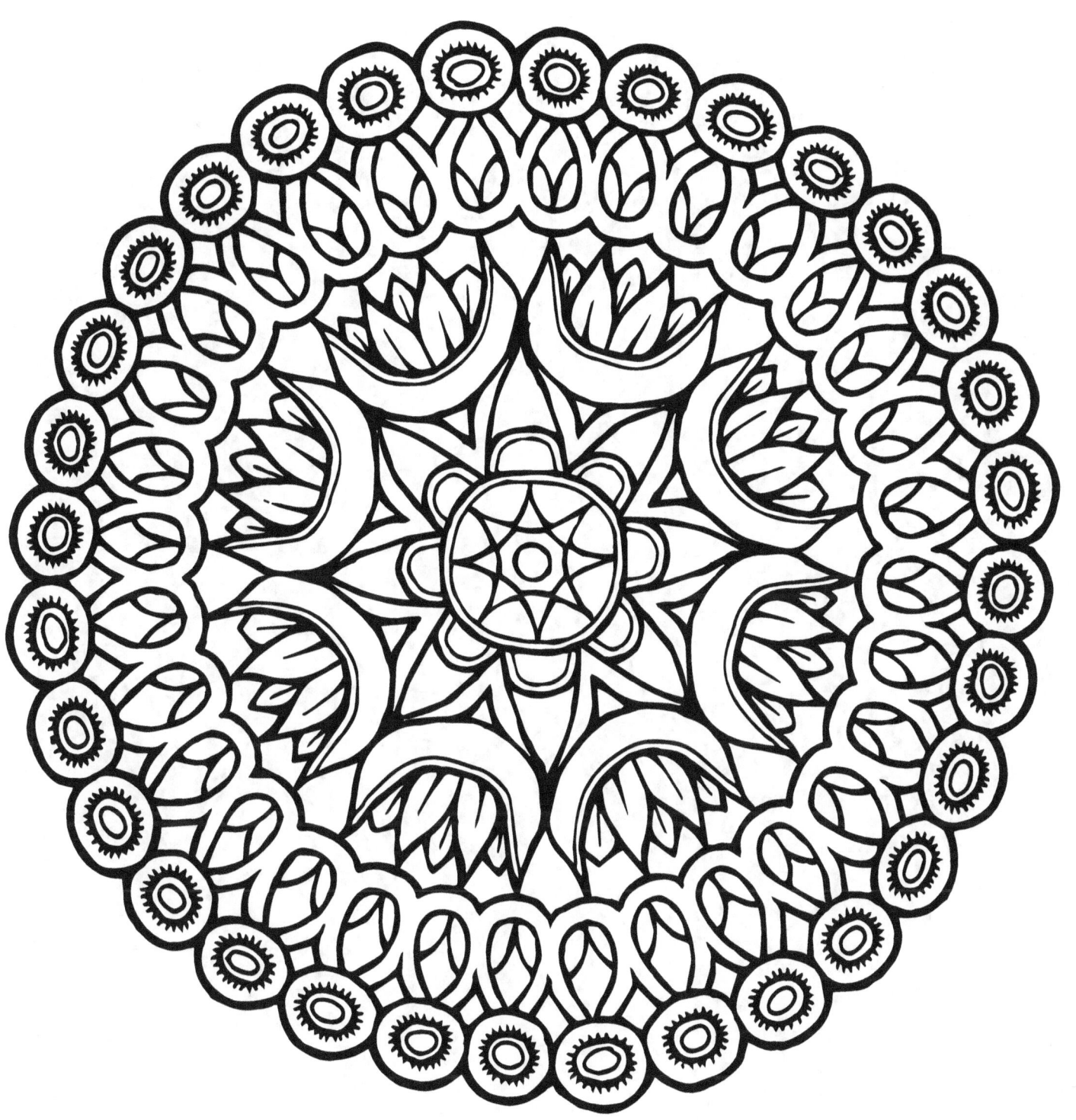

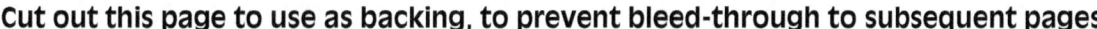 **Cut out this page to use as backing, to prevent bleed-through to subsequent pages**

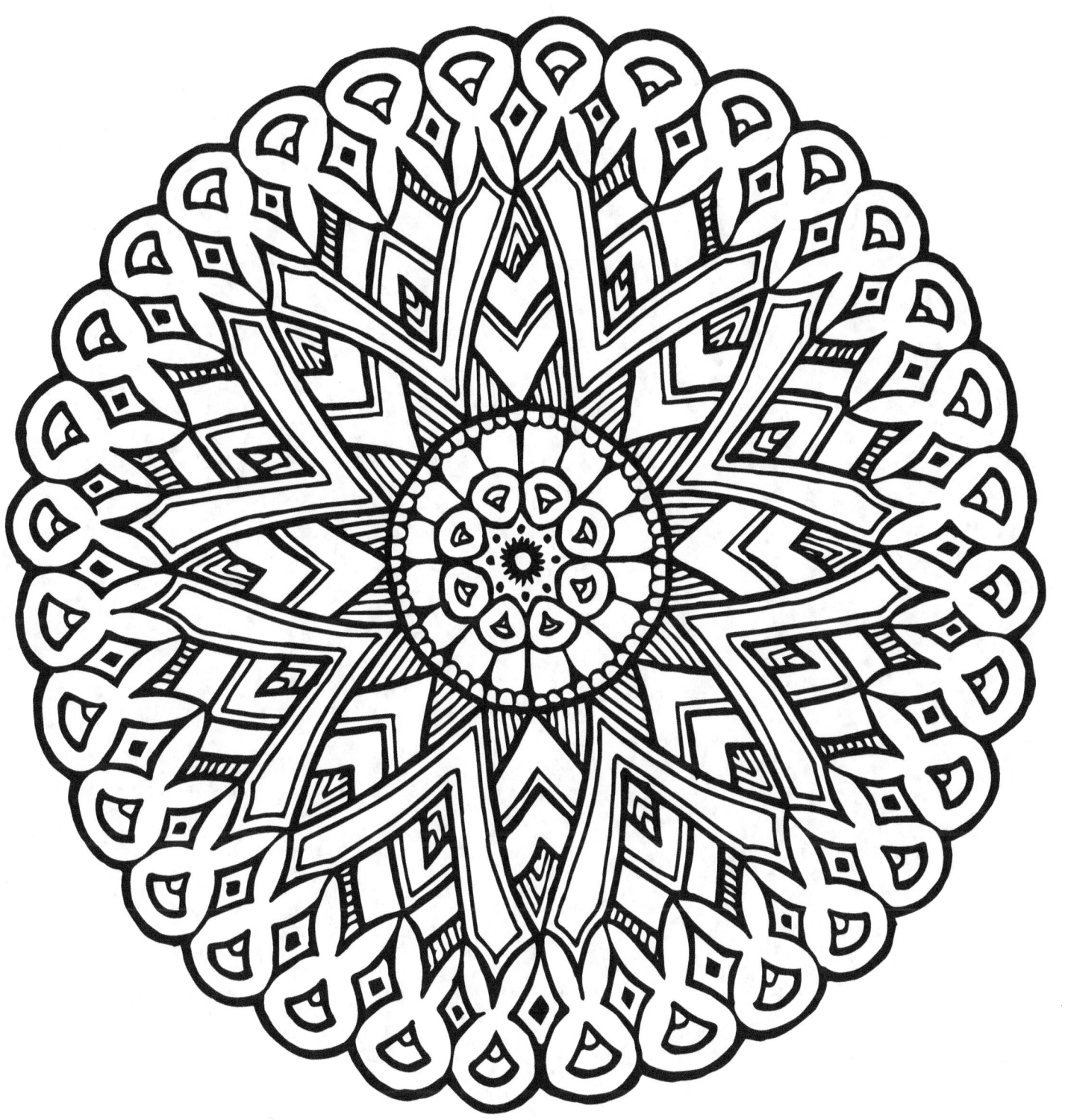

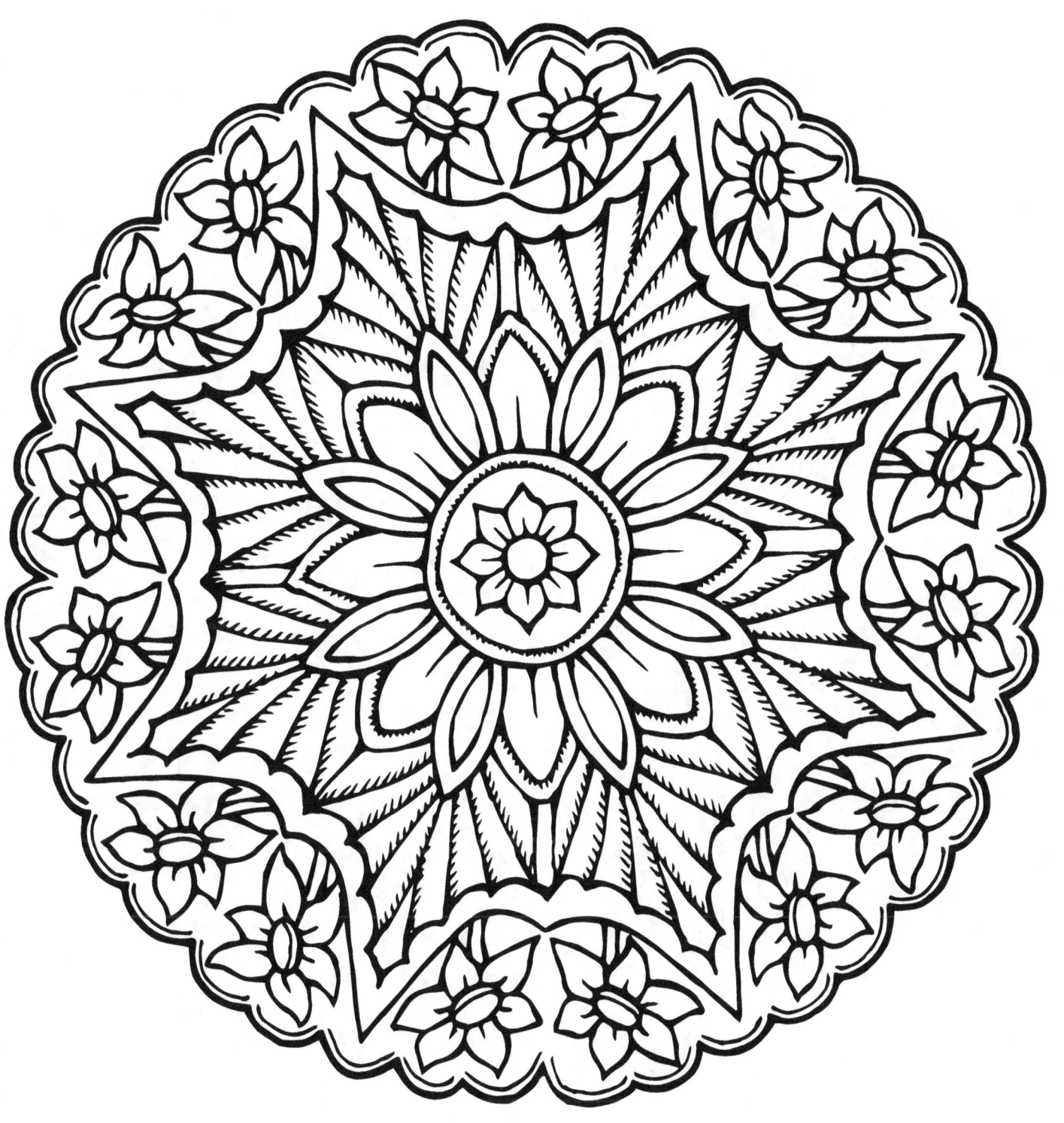

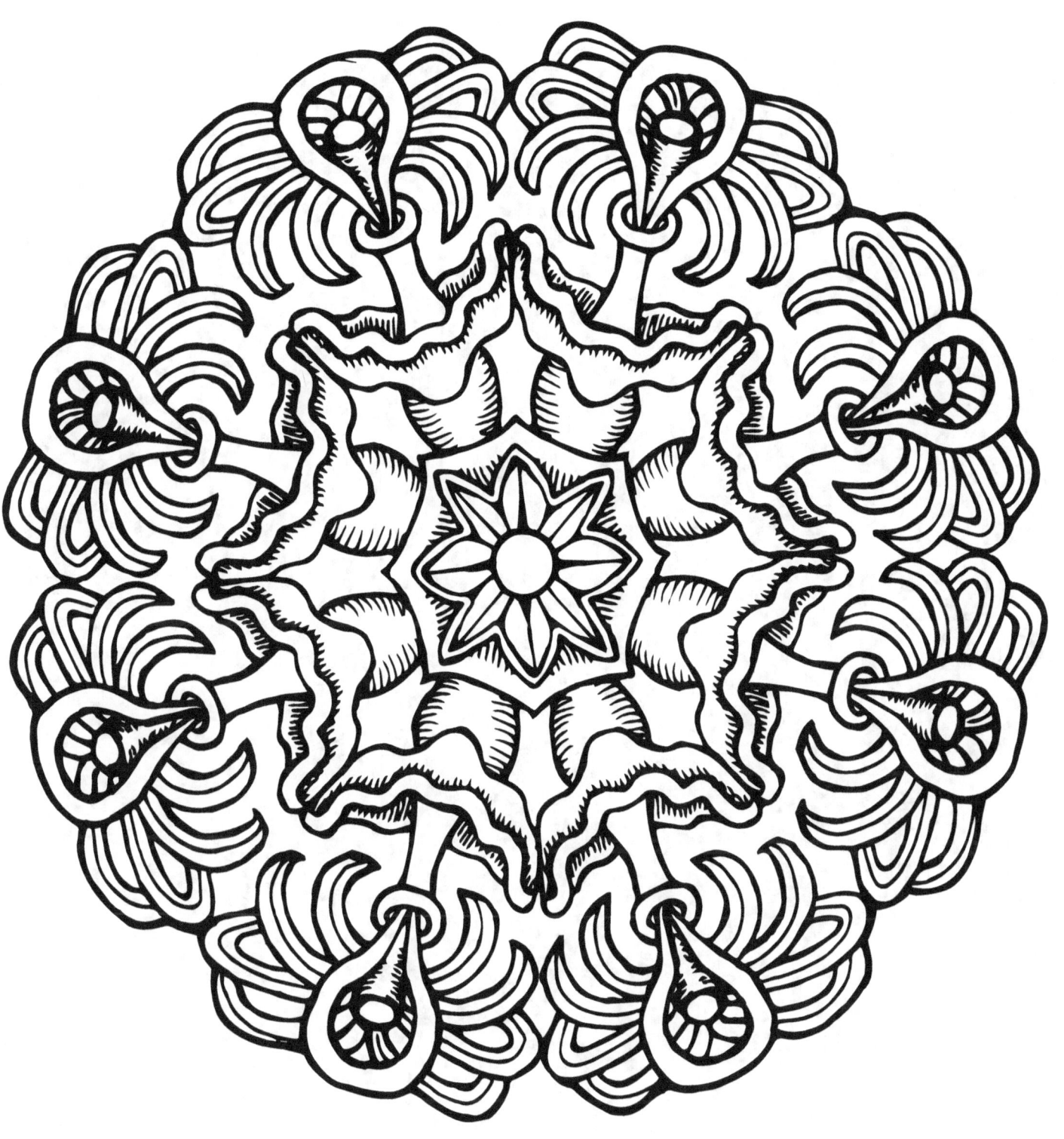

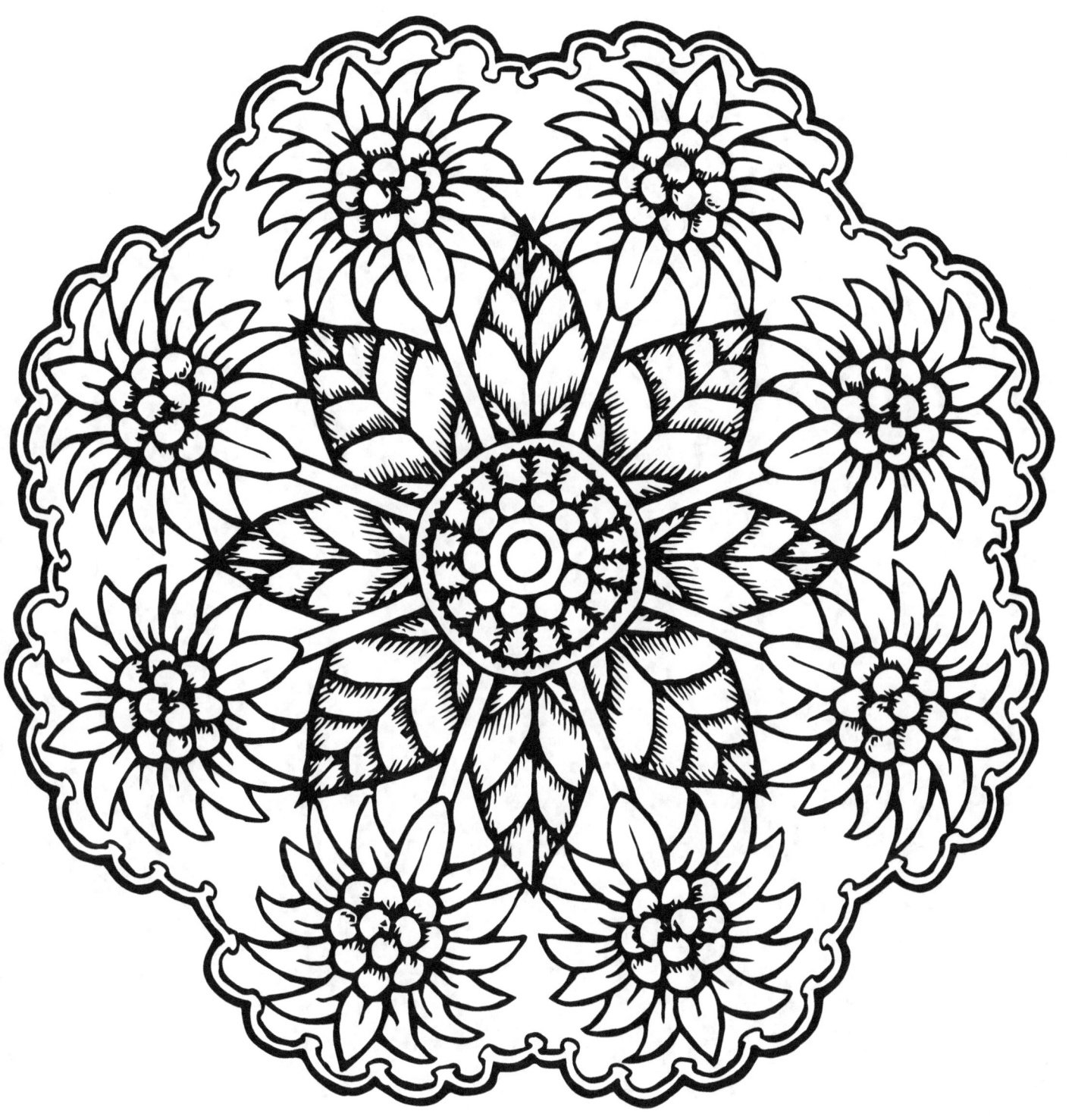

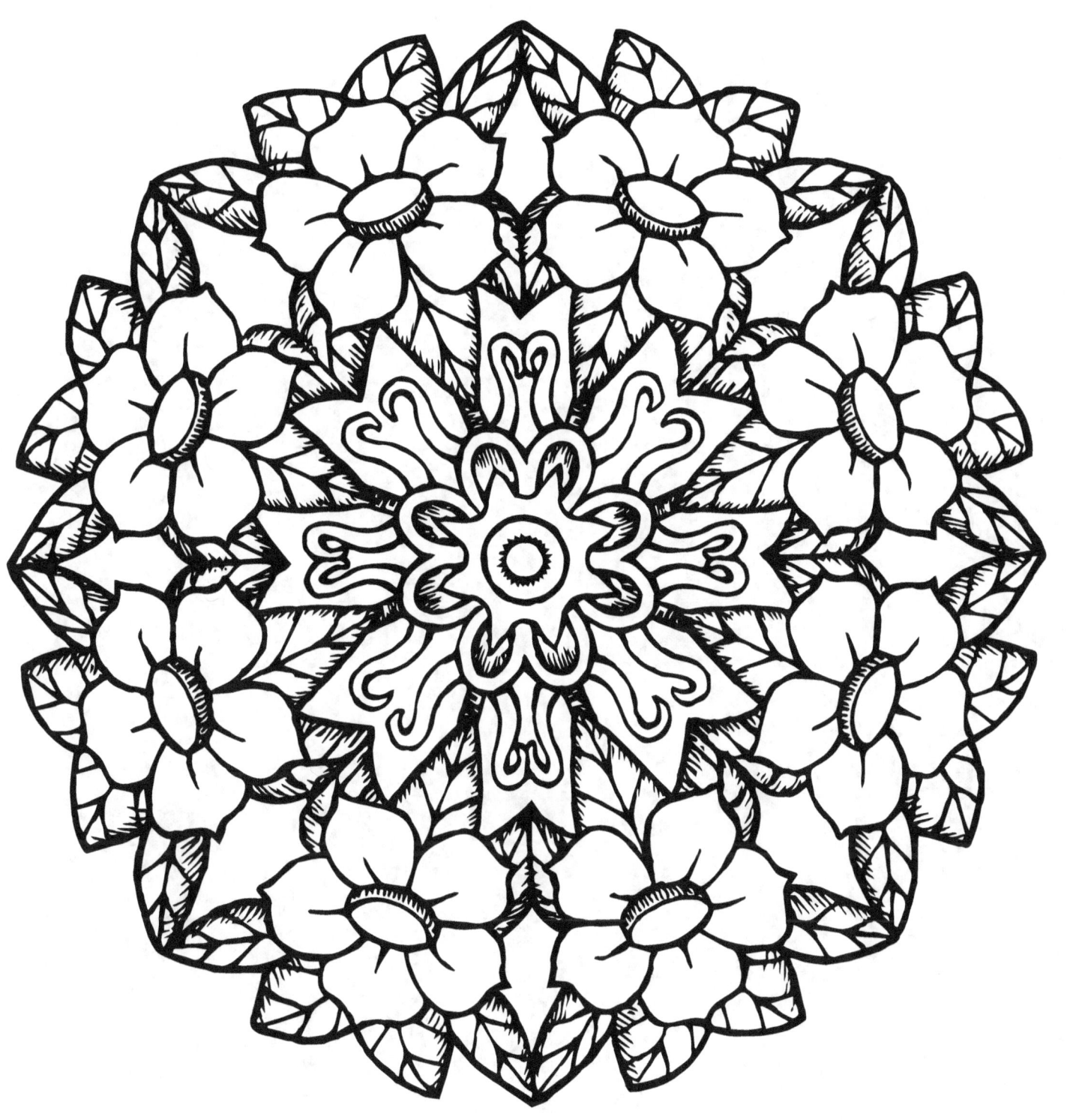

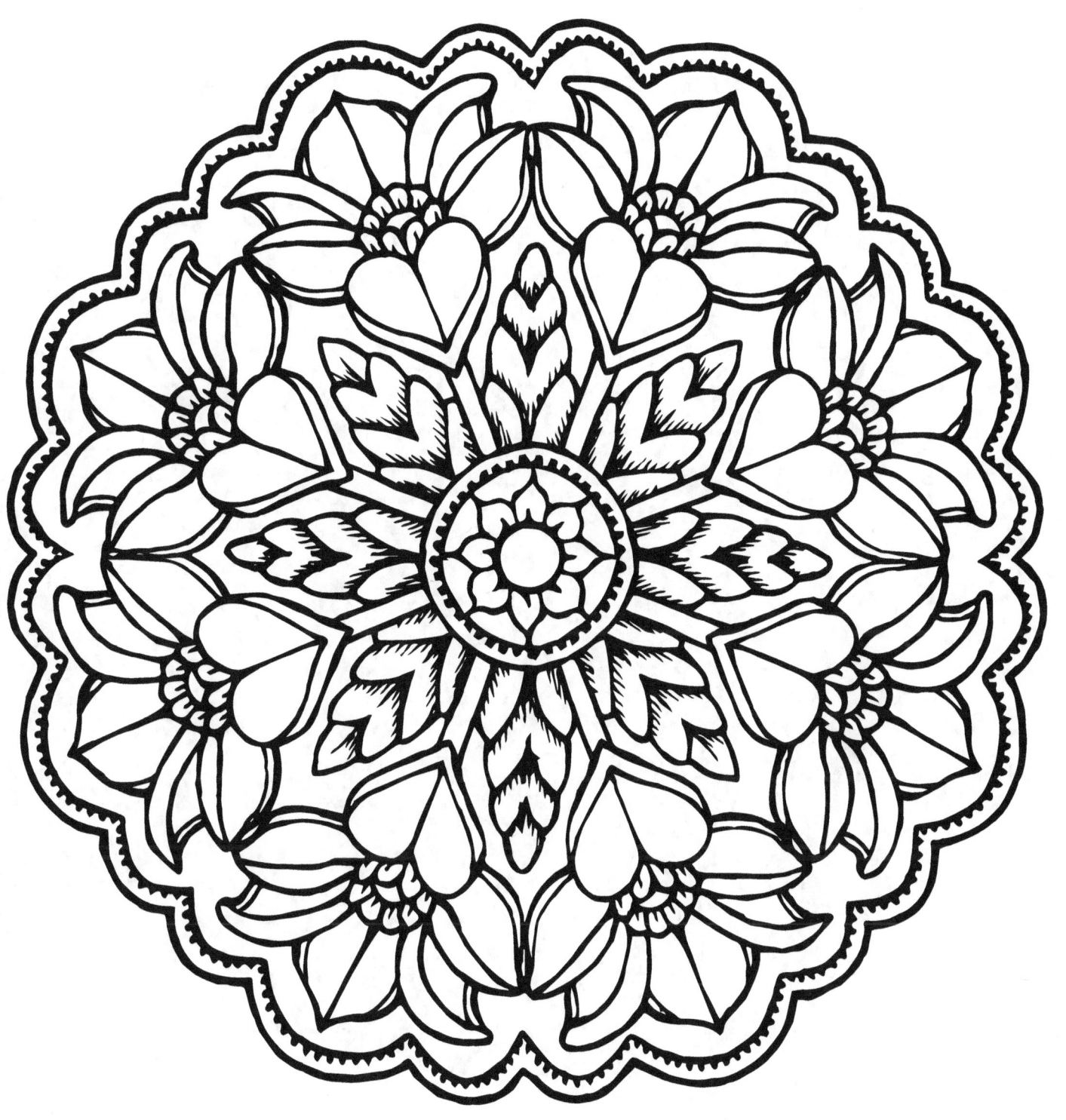

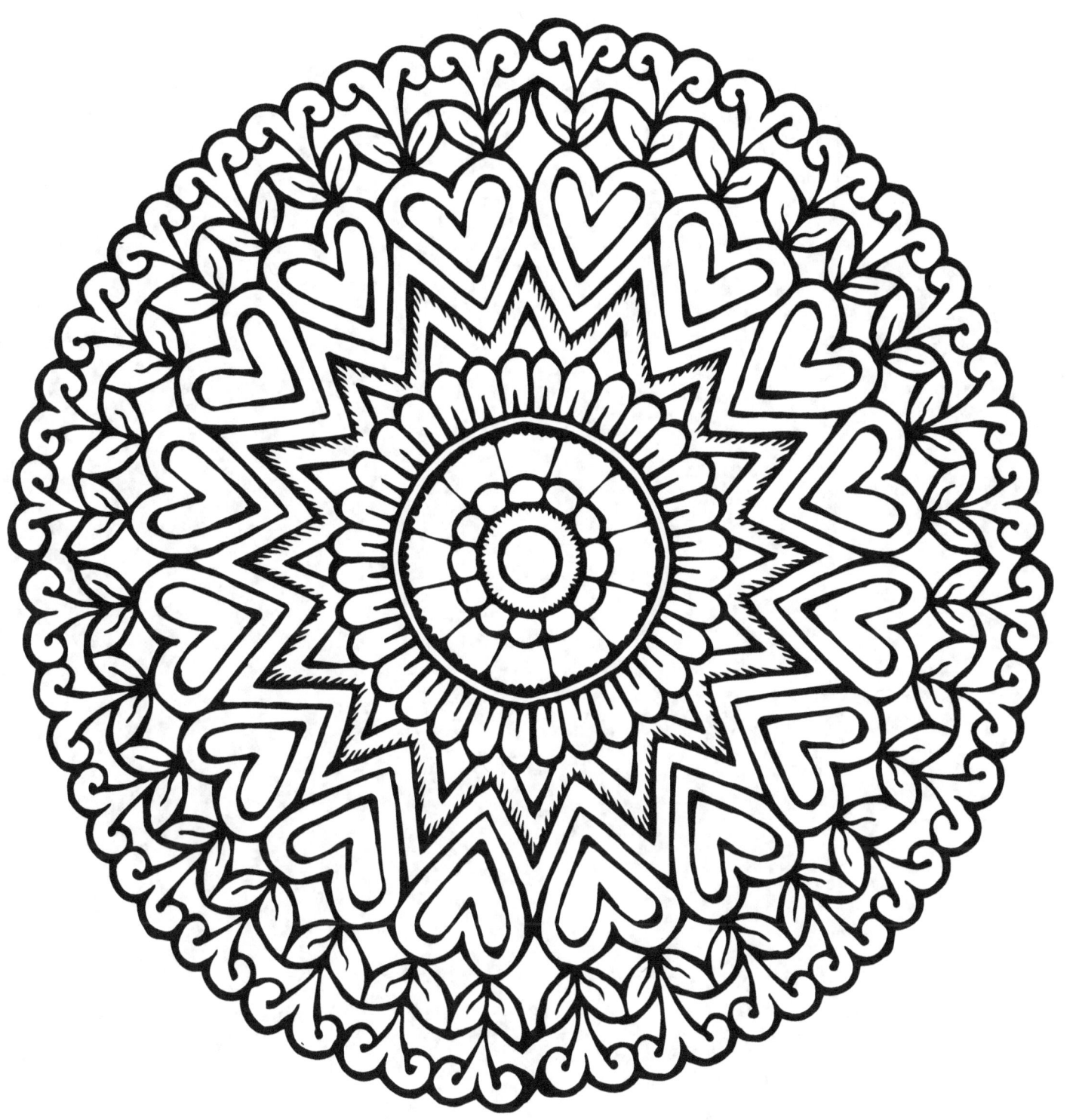

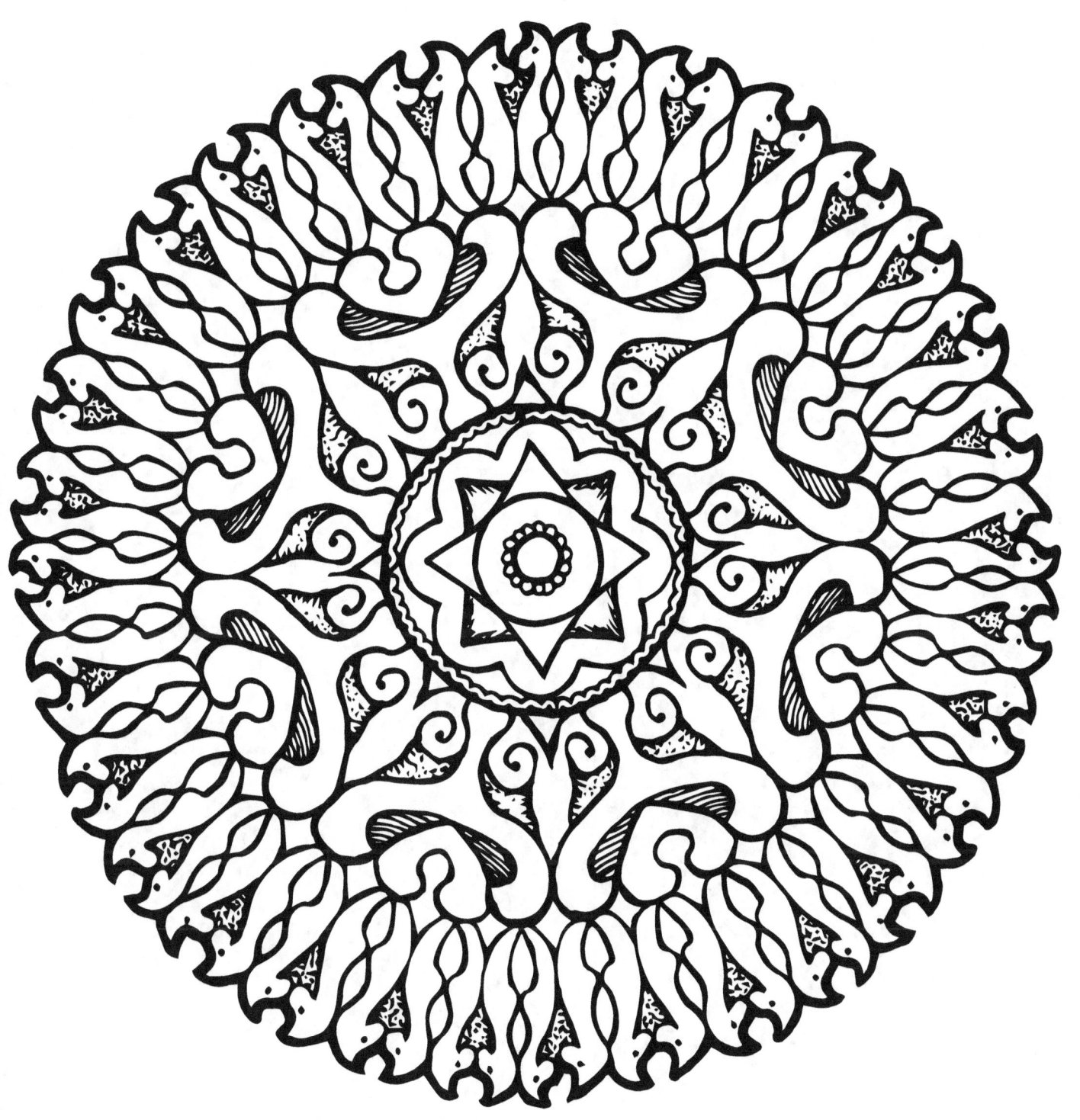

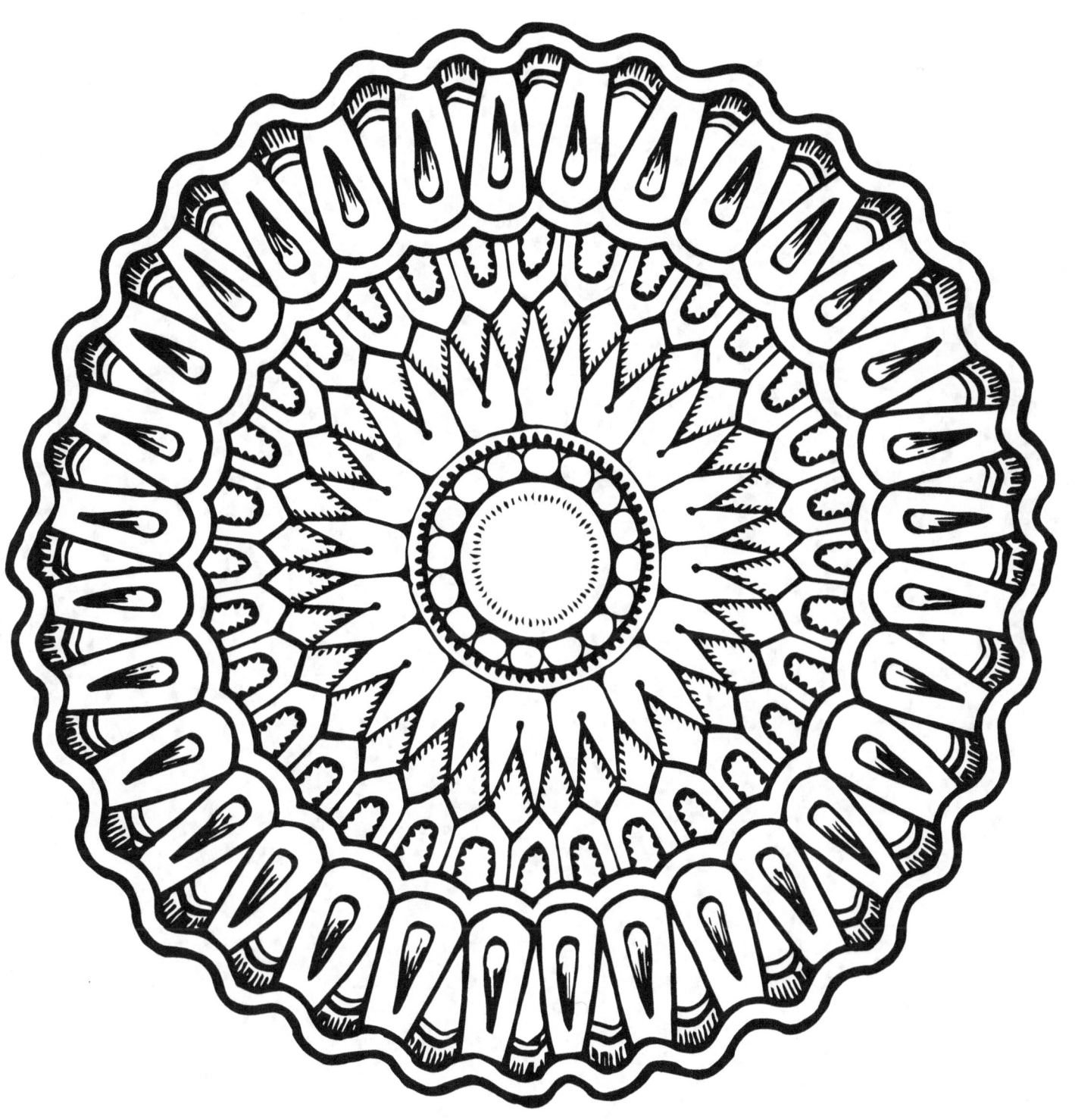

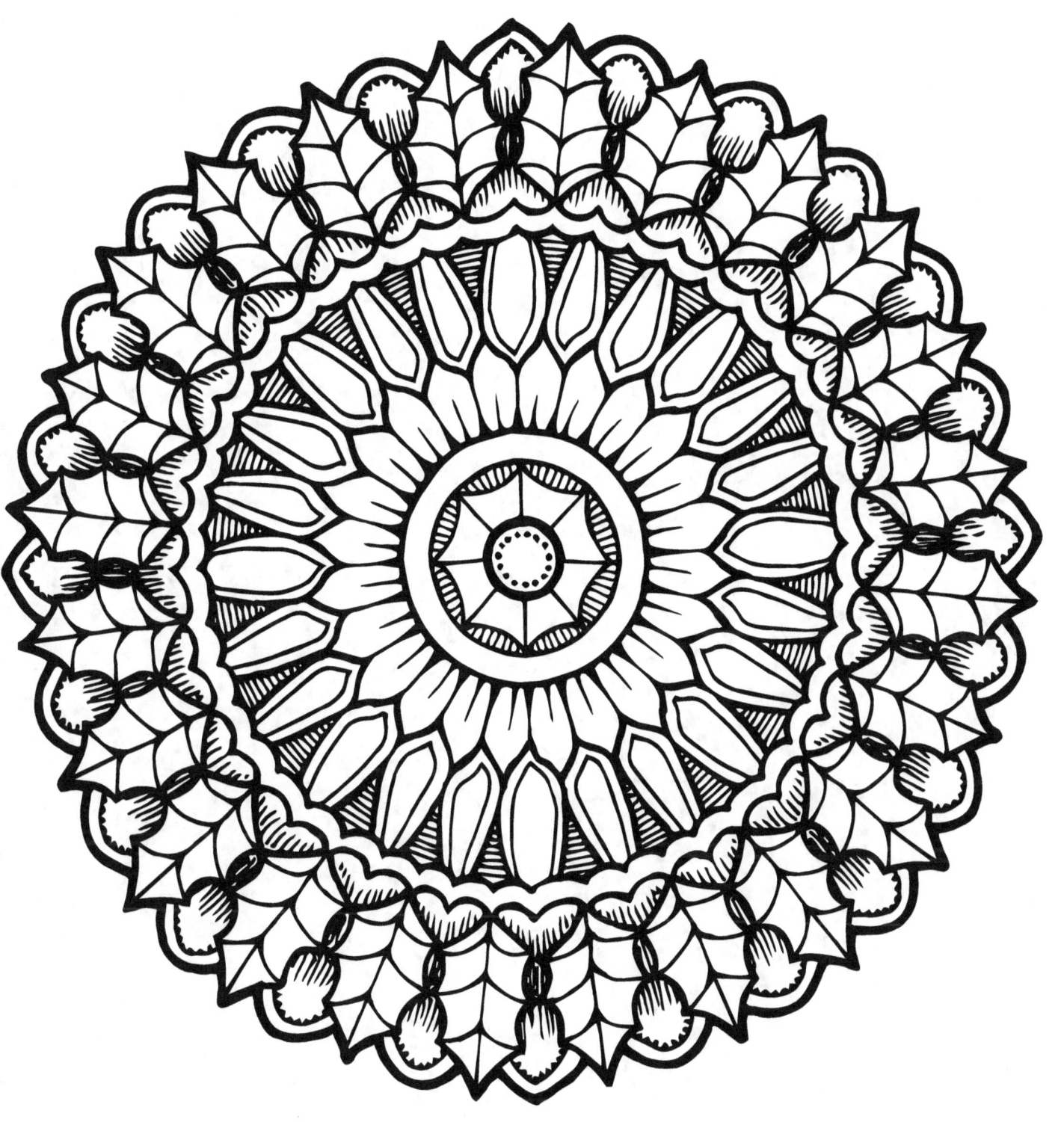

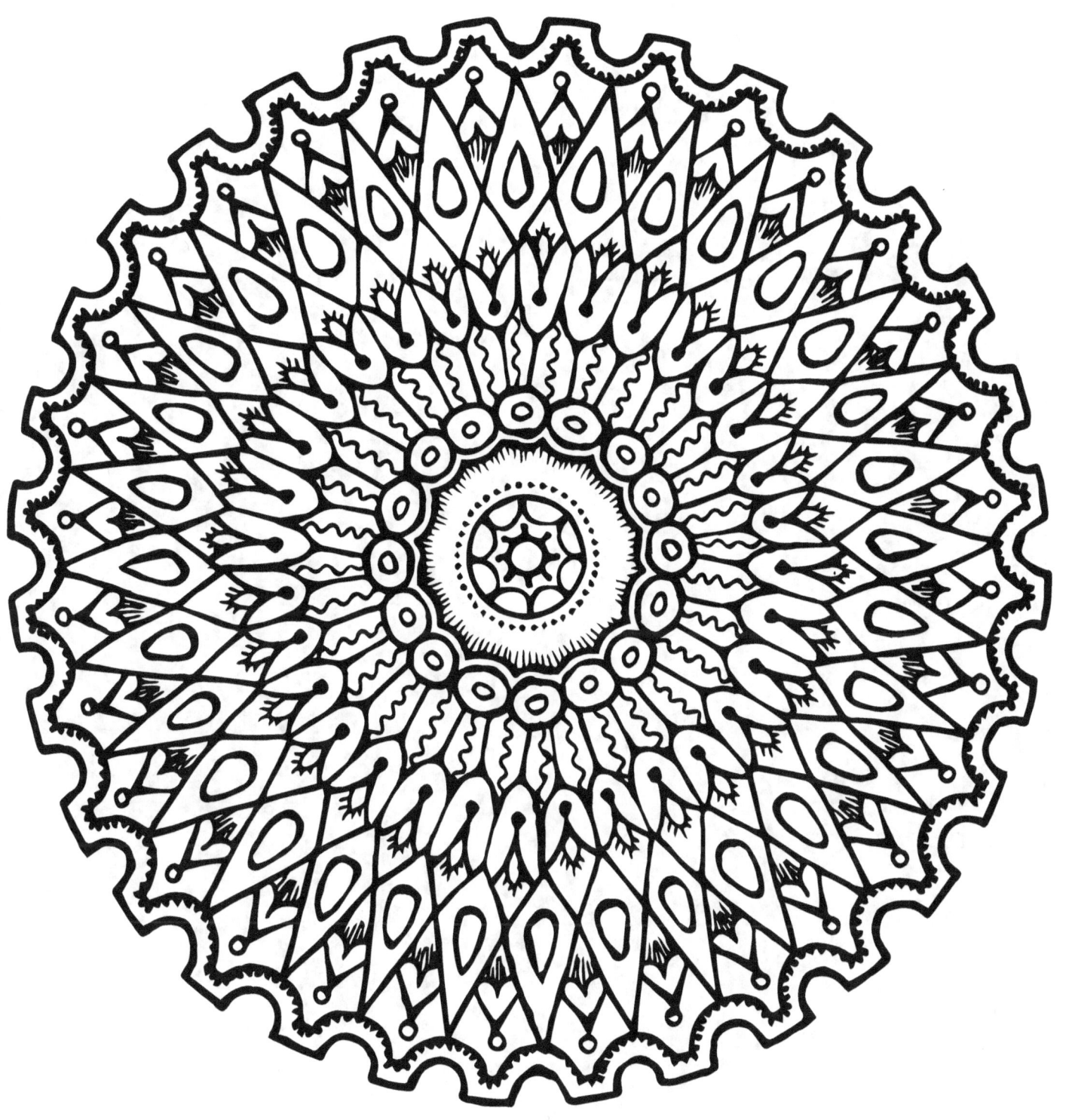

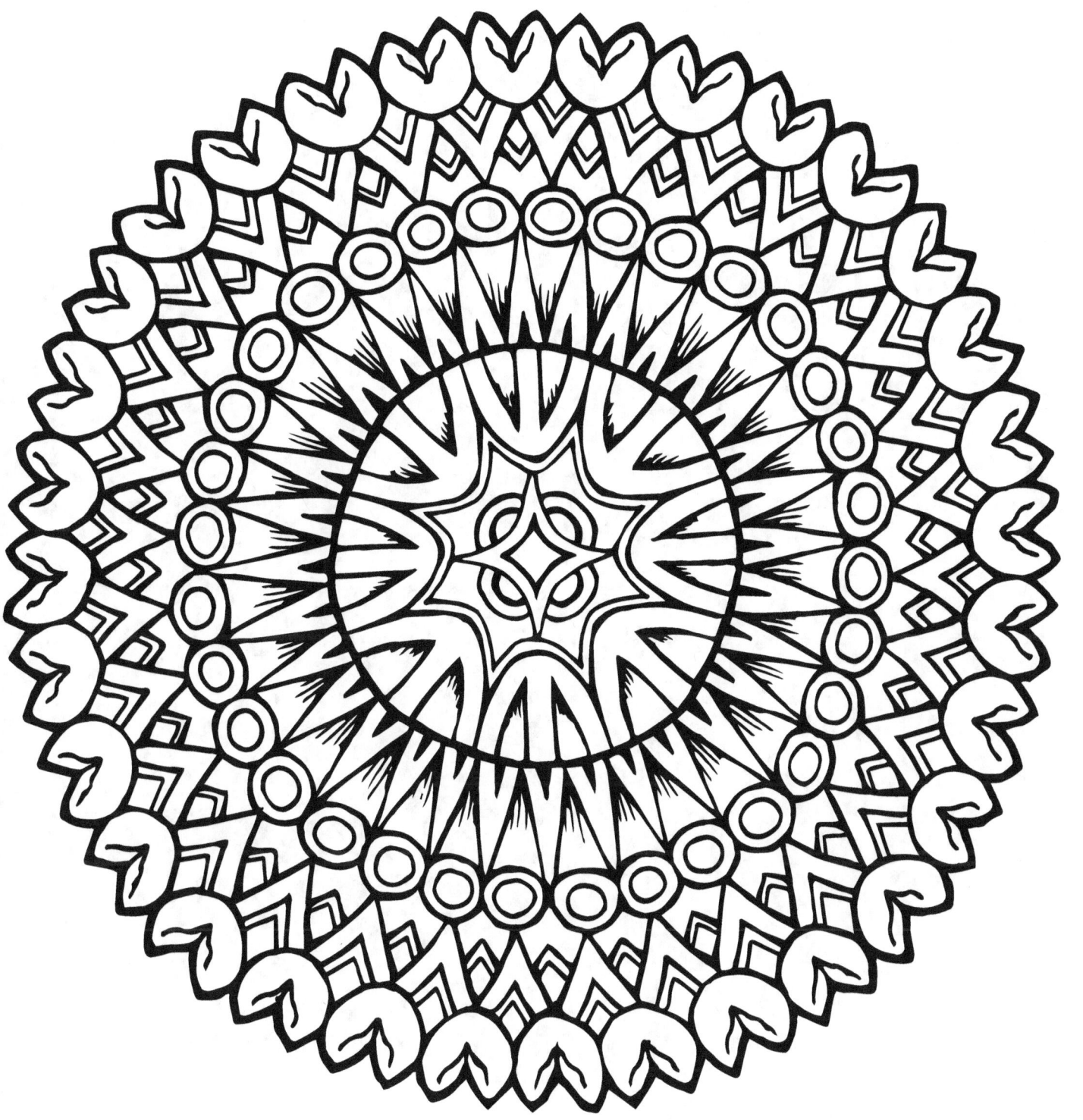

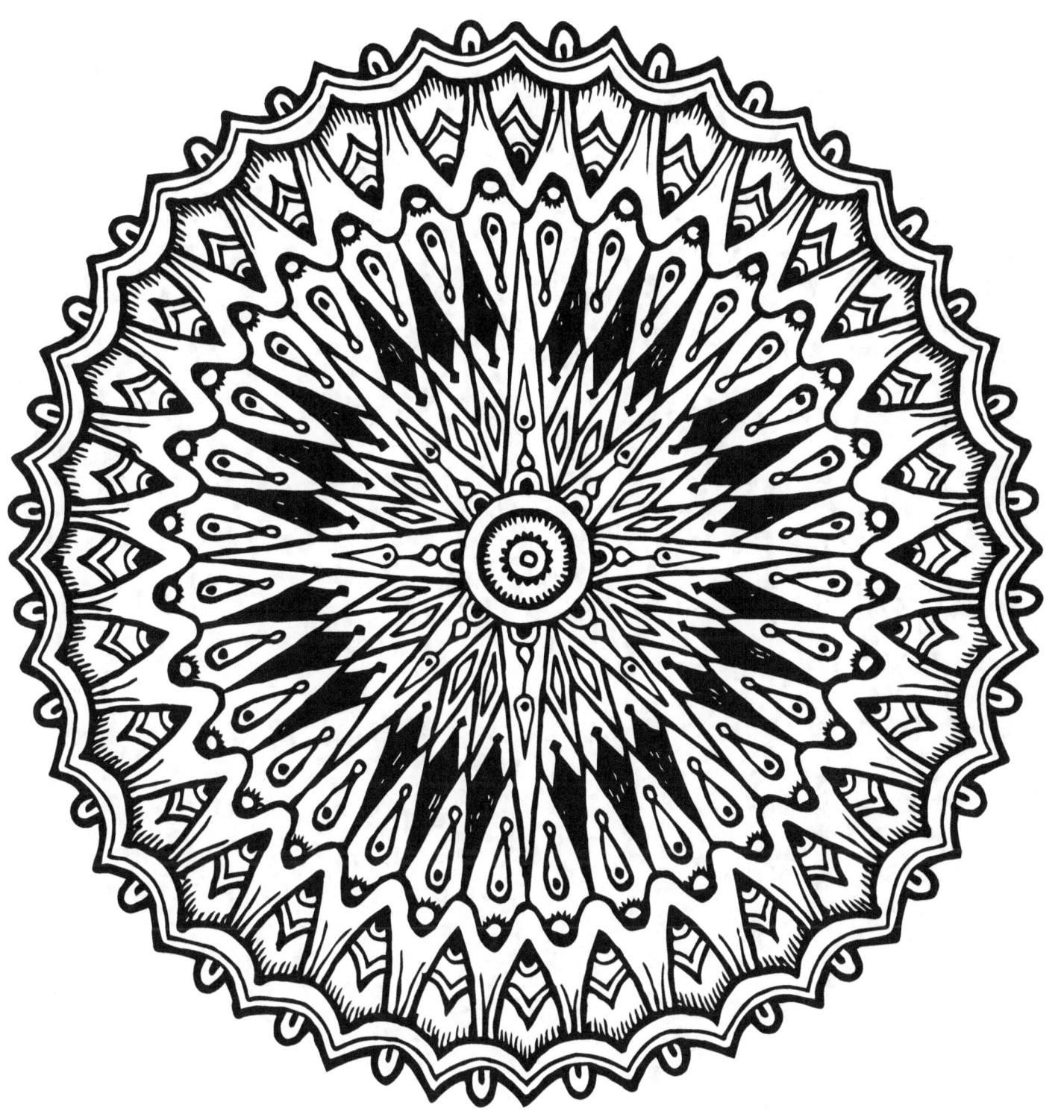

14

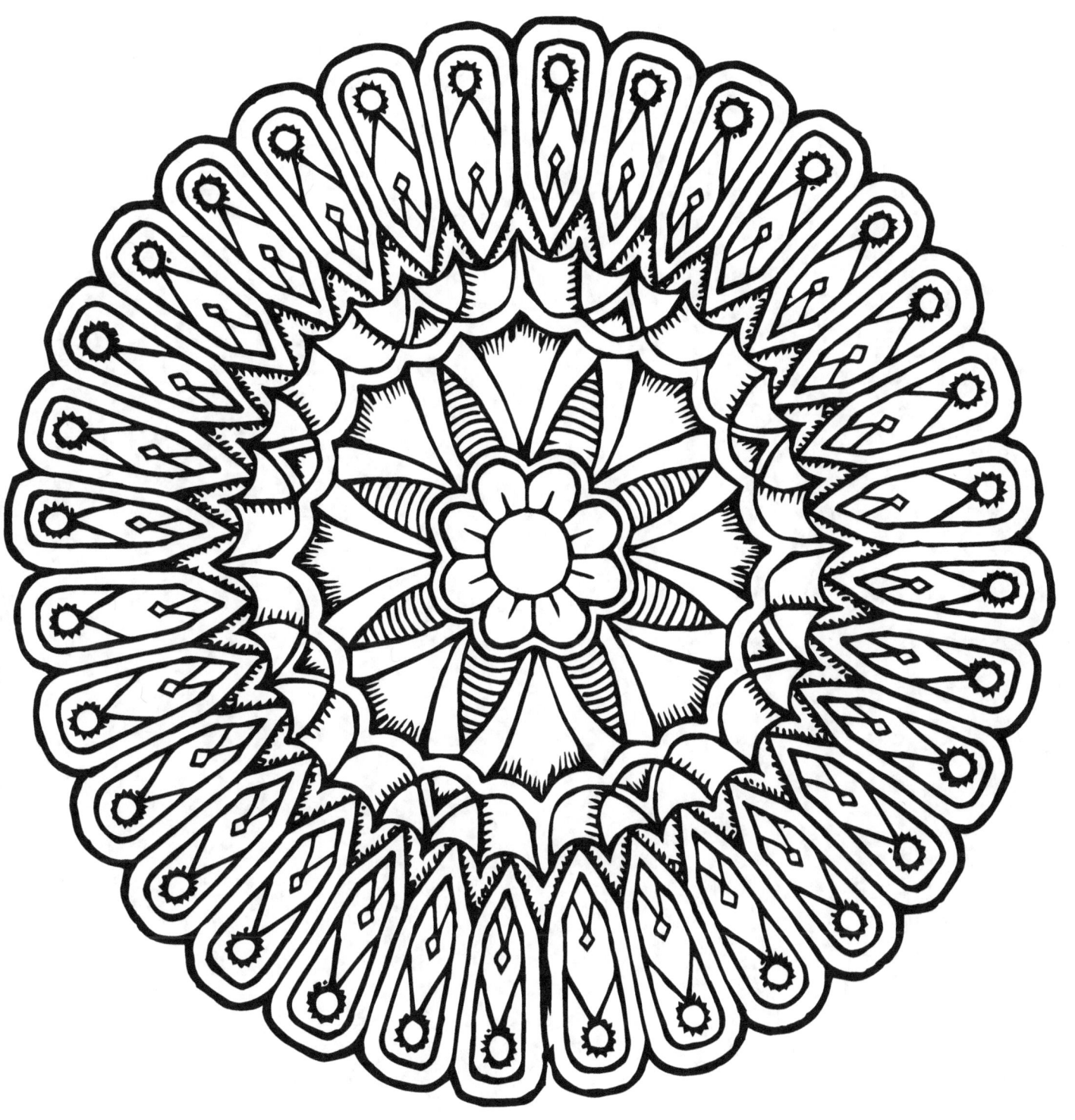

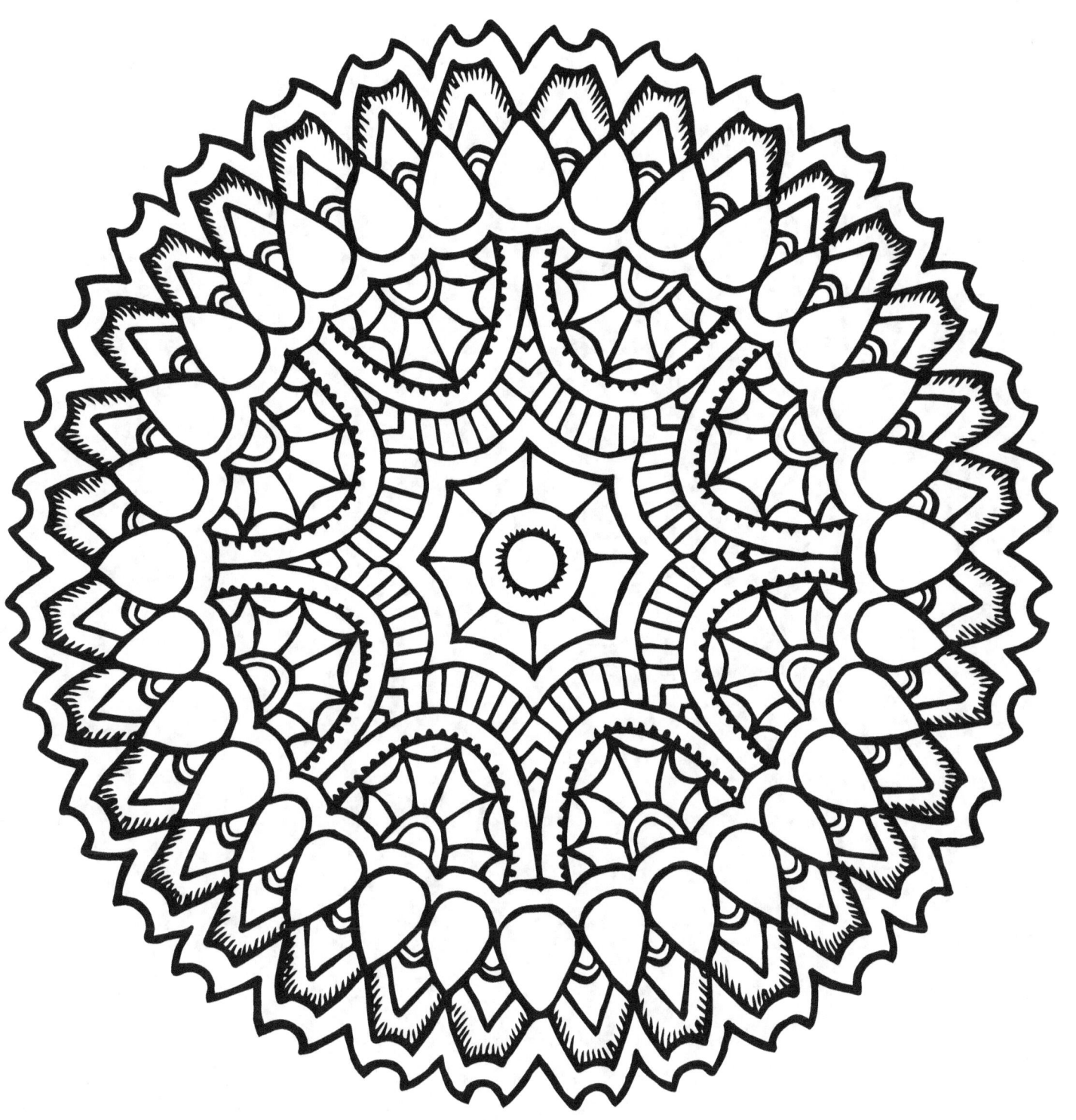

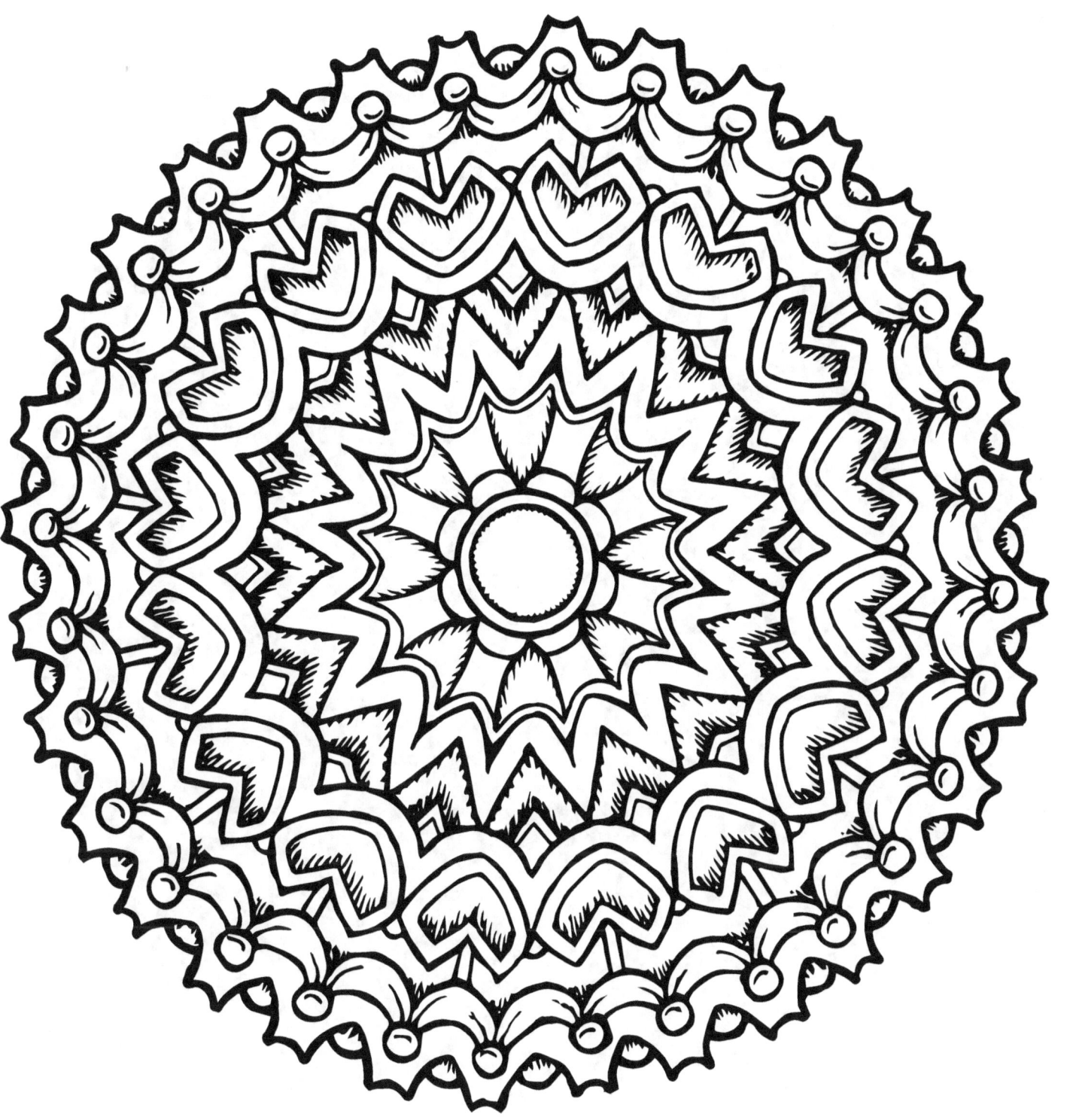

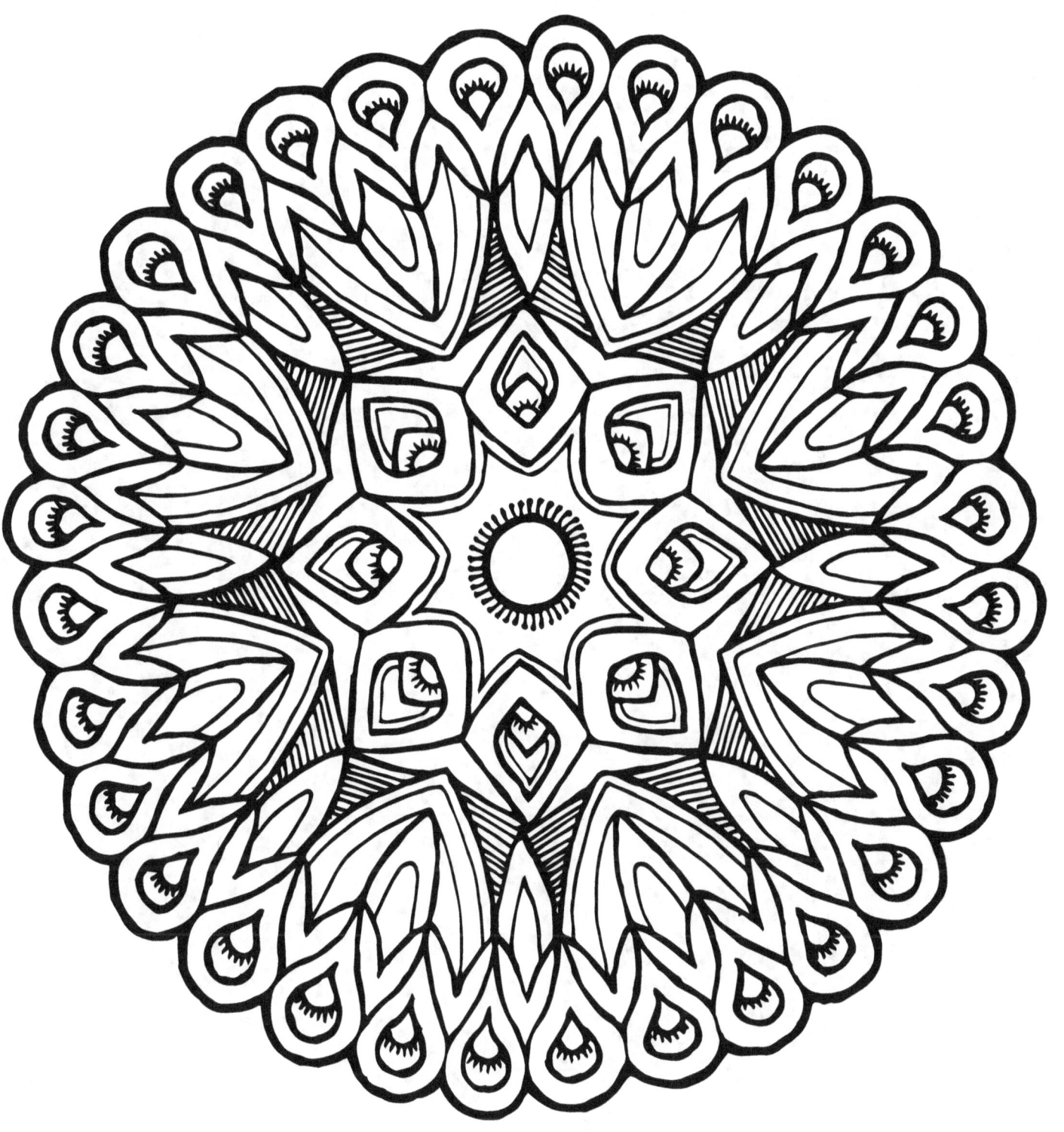

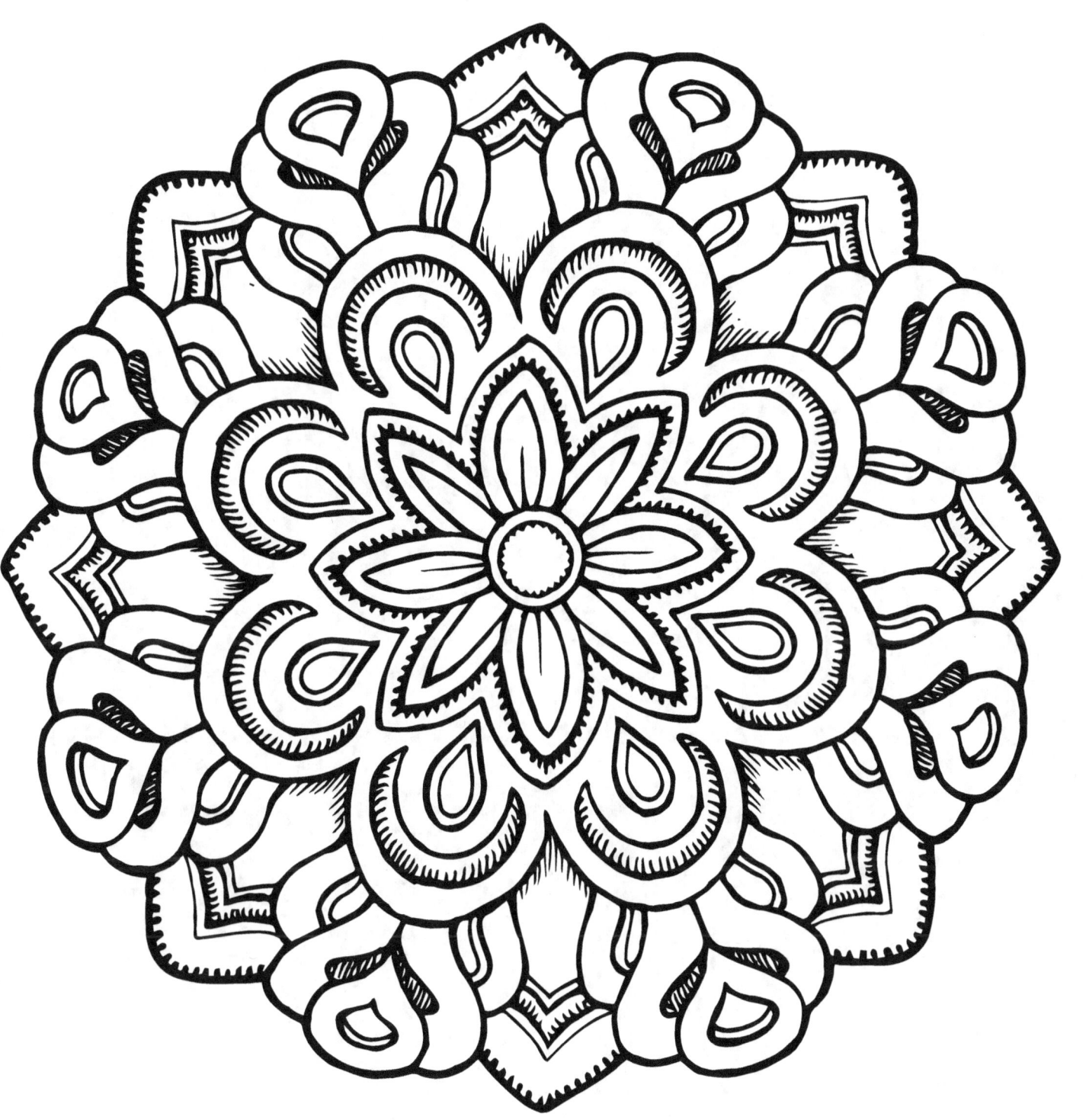

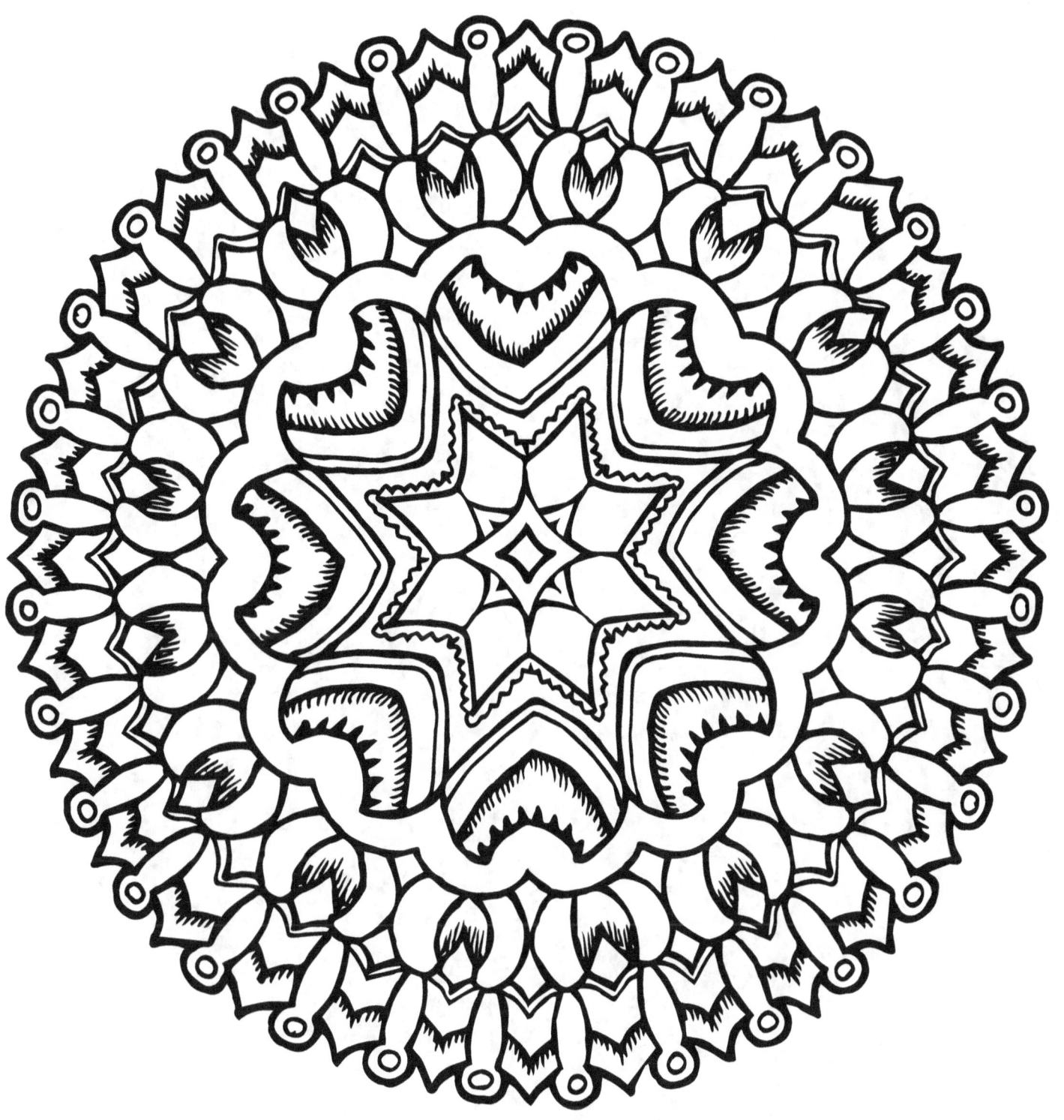

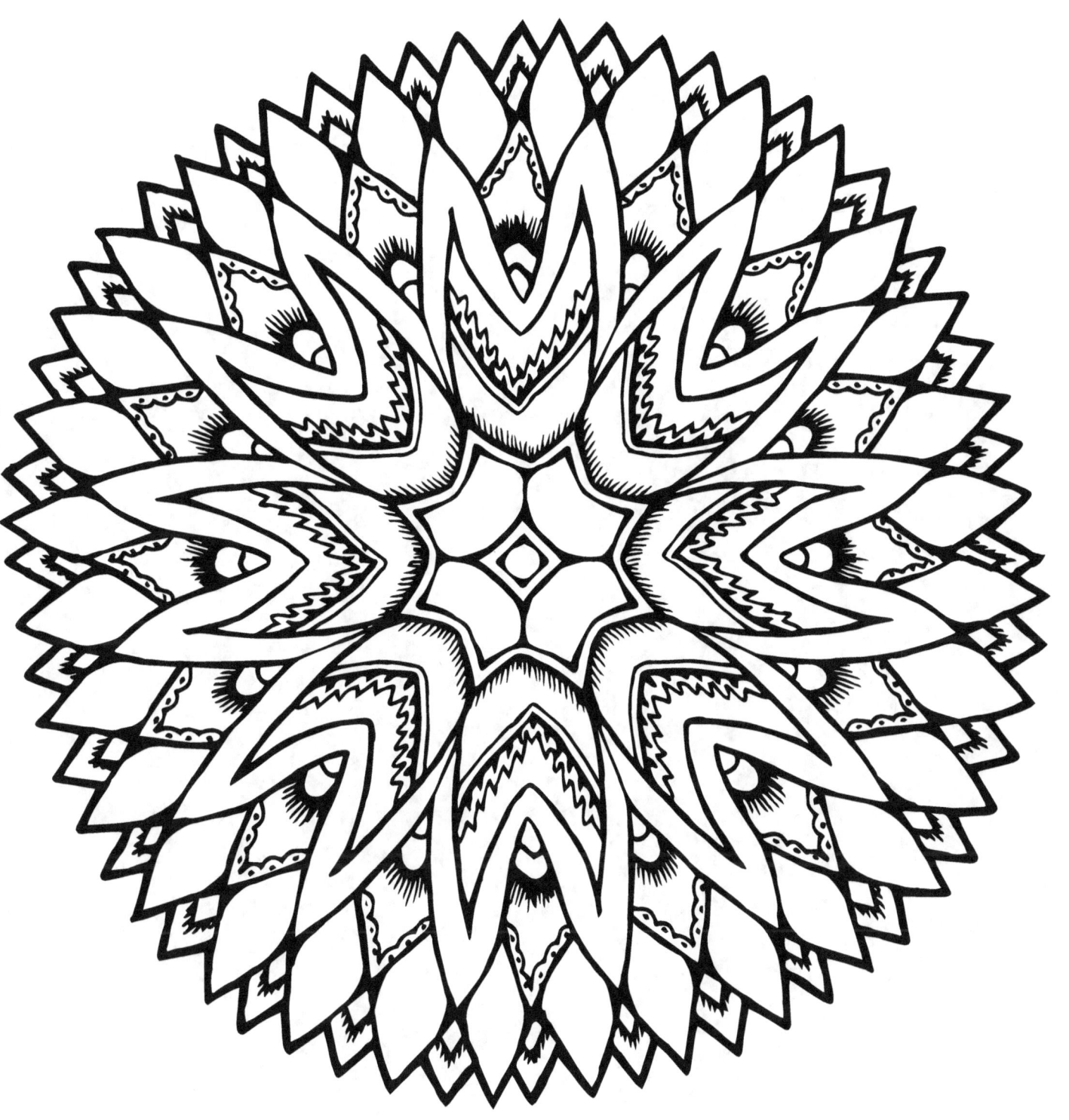

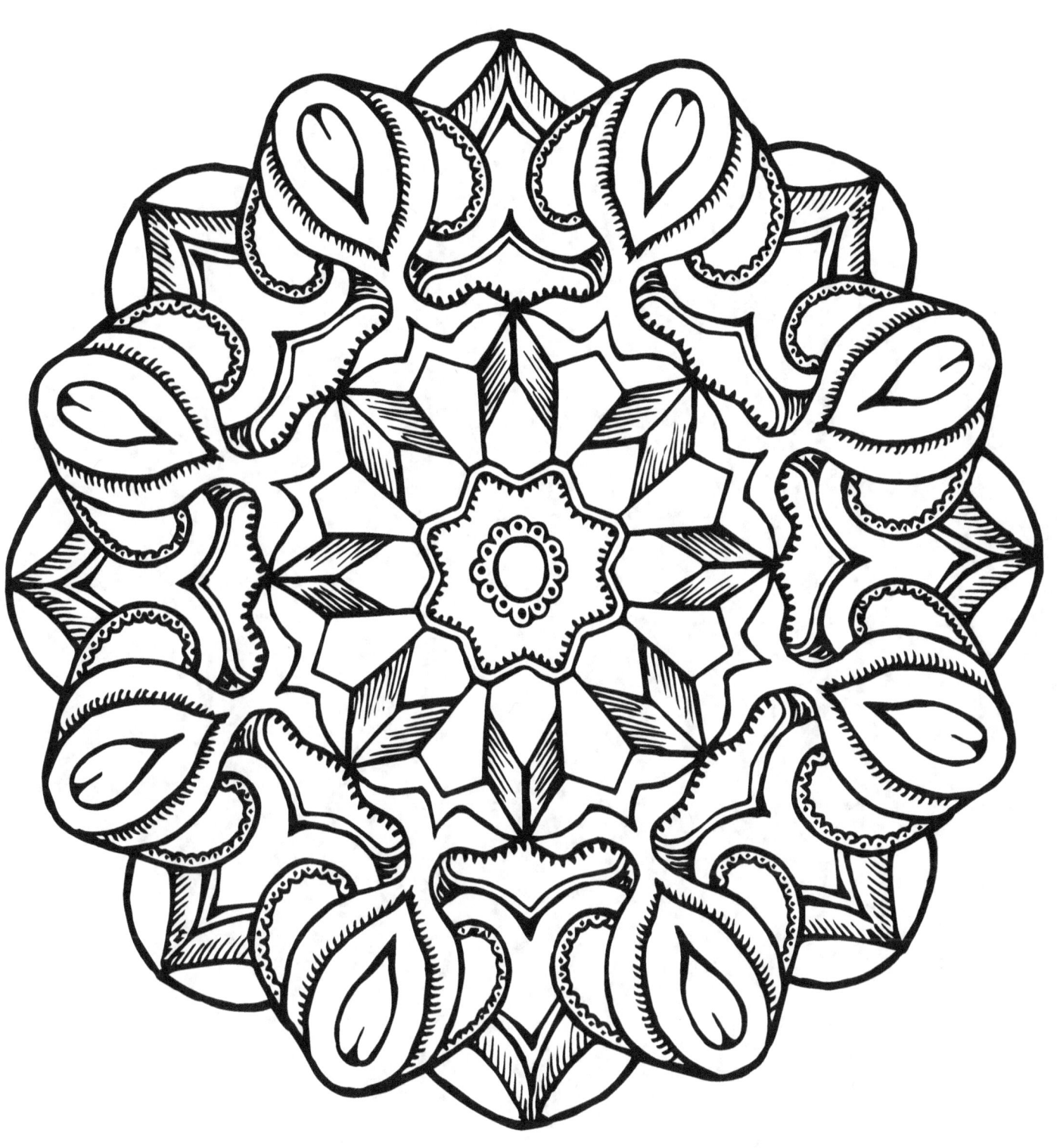

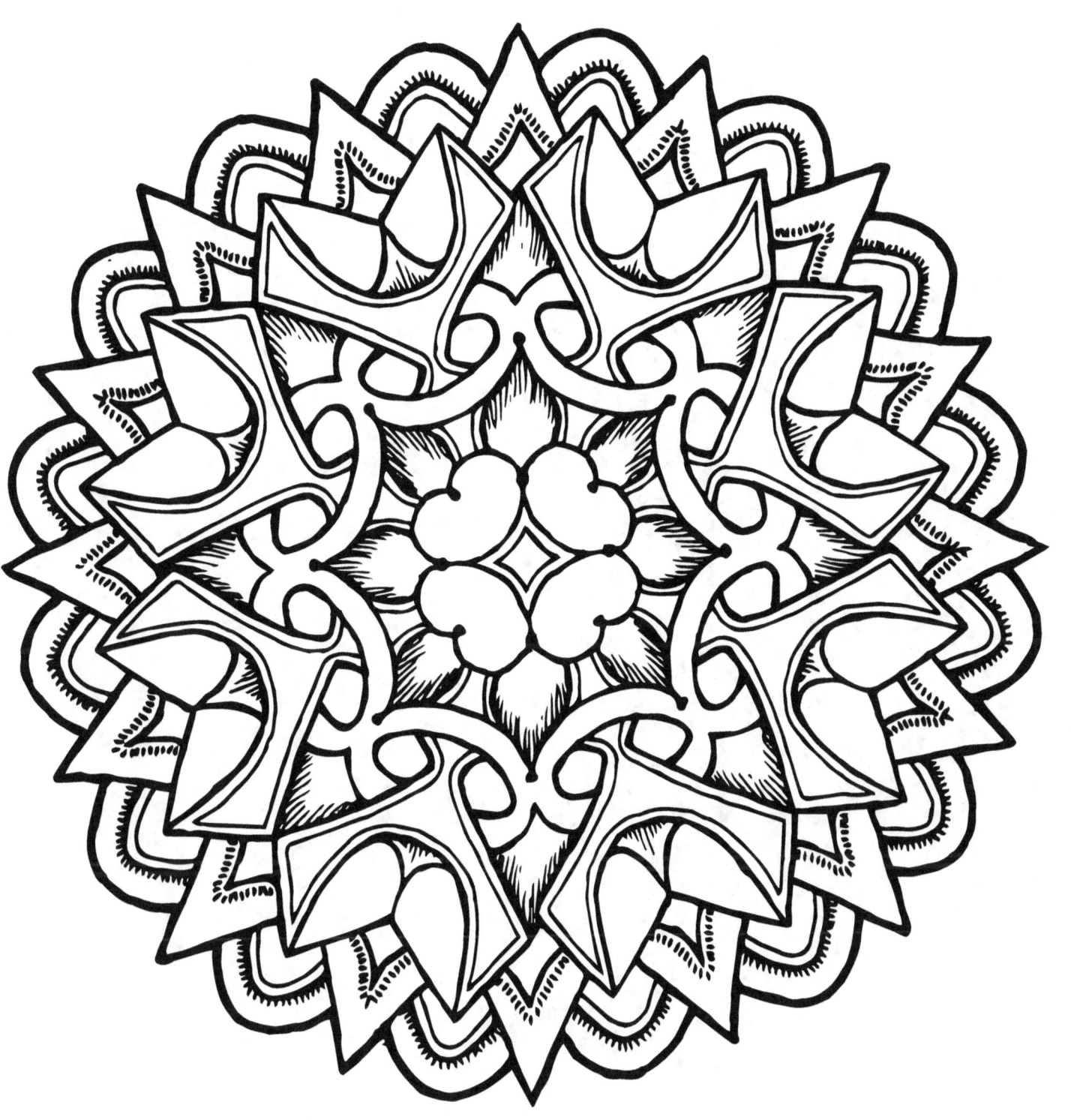

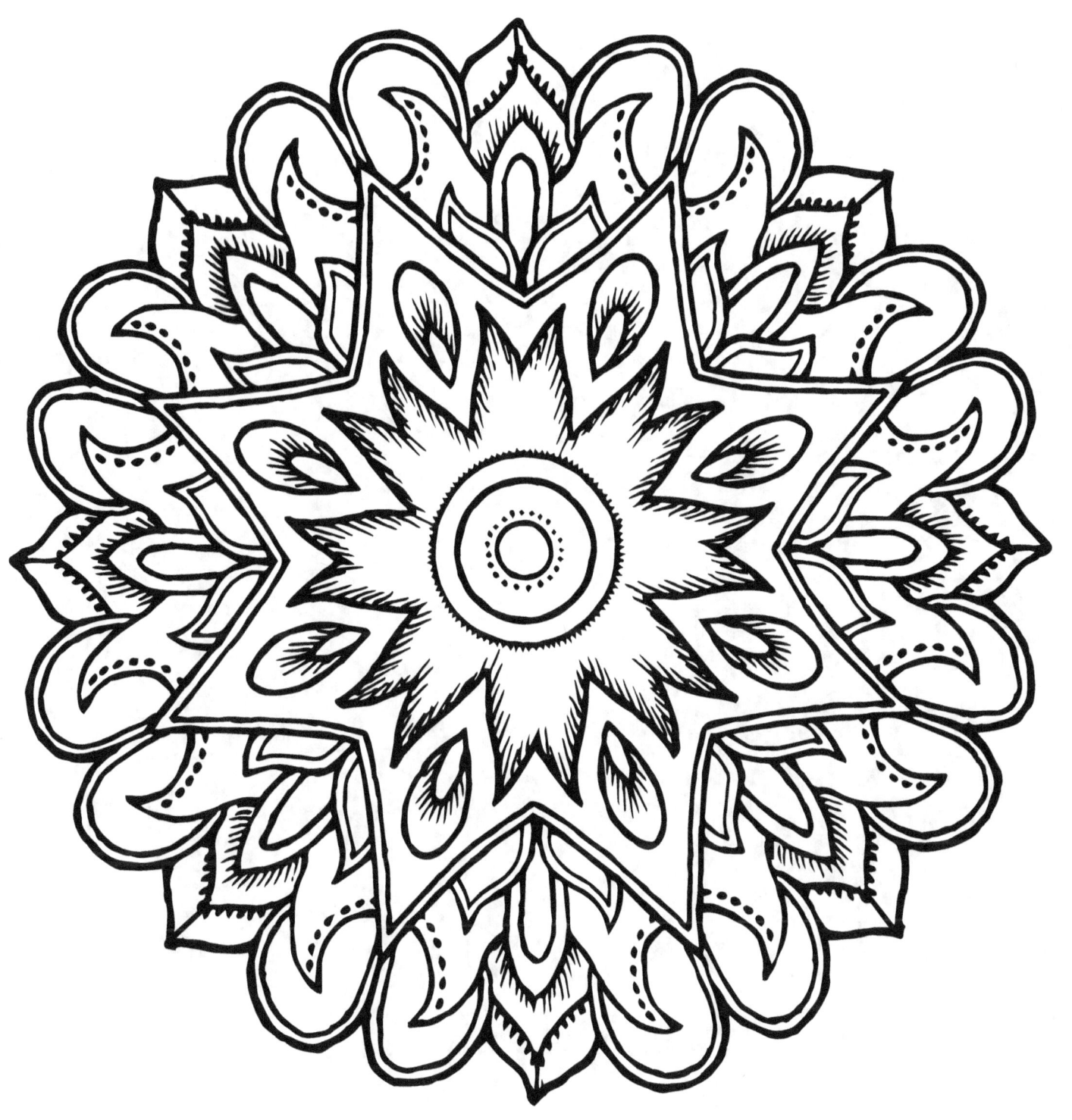

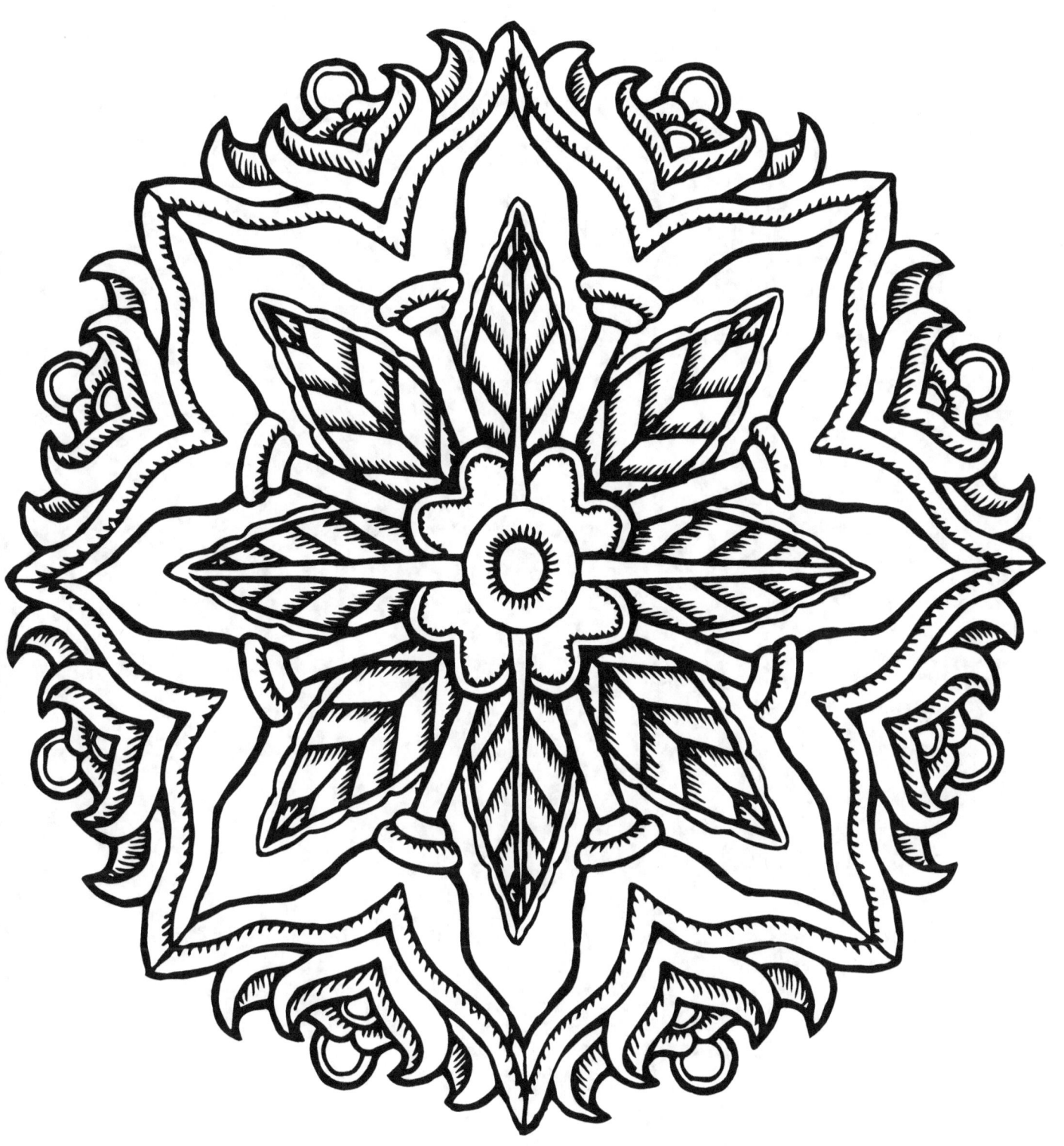

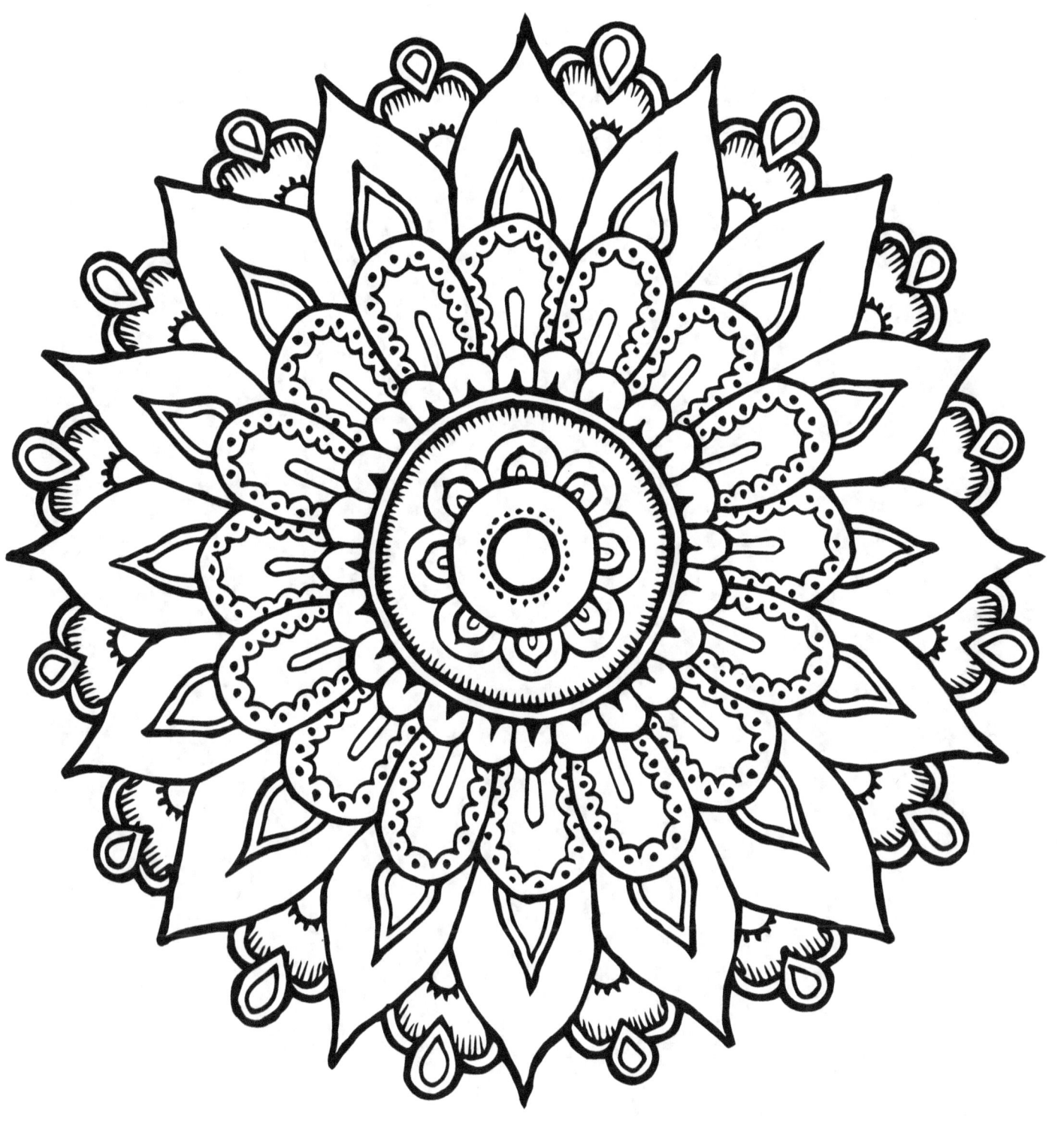

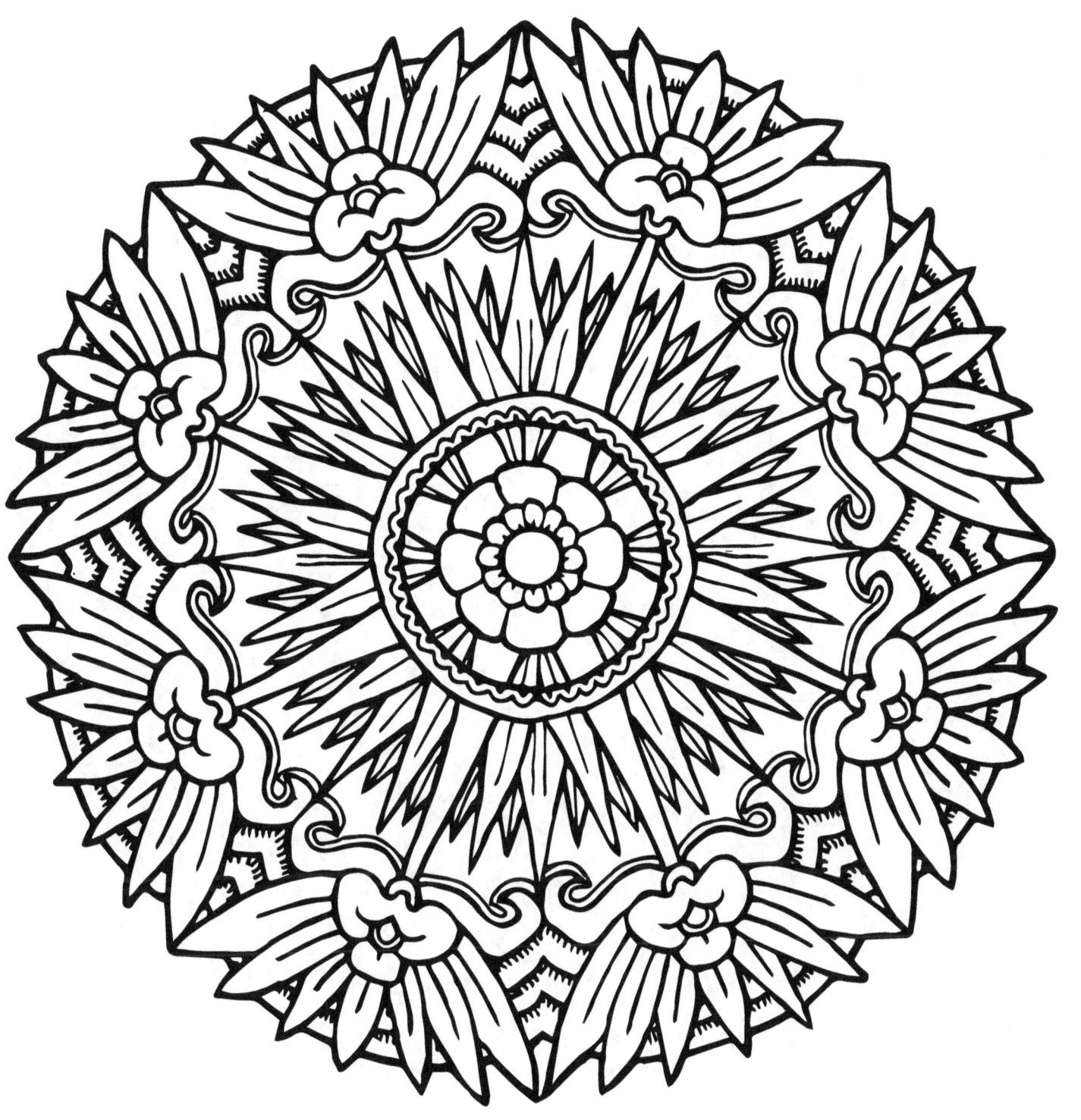

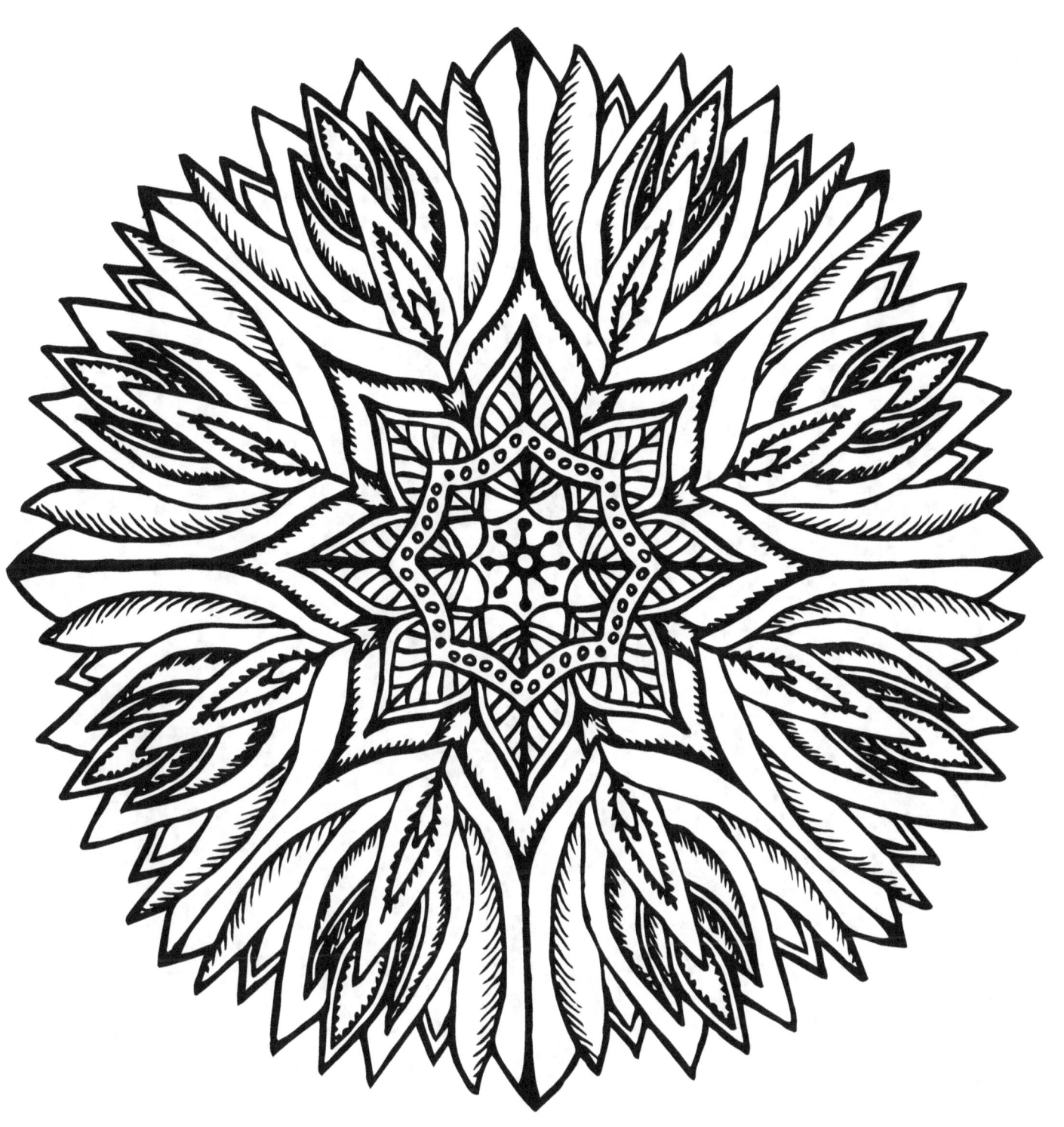

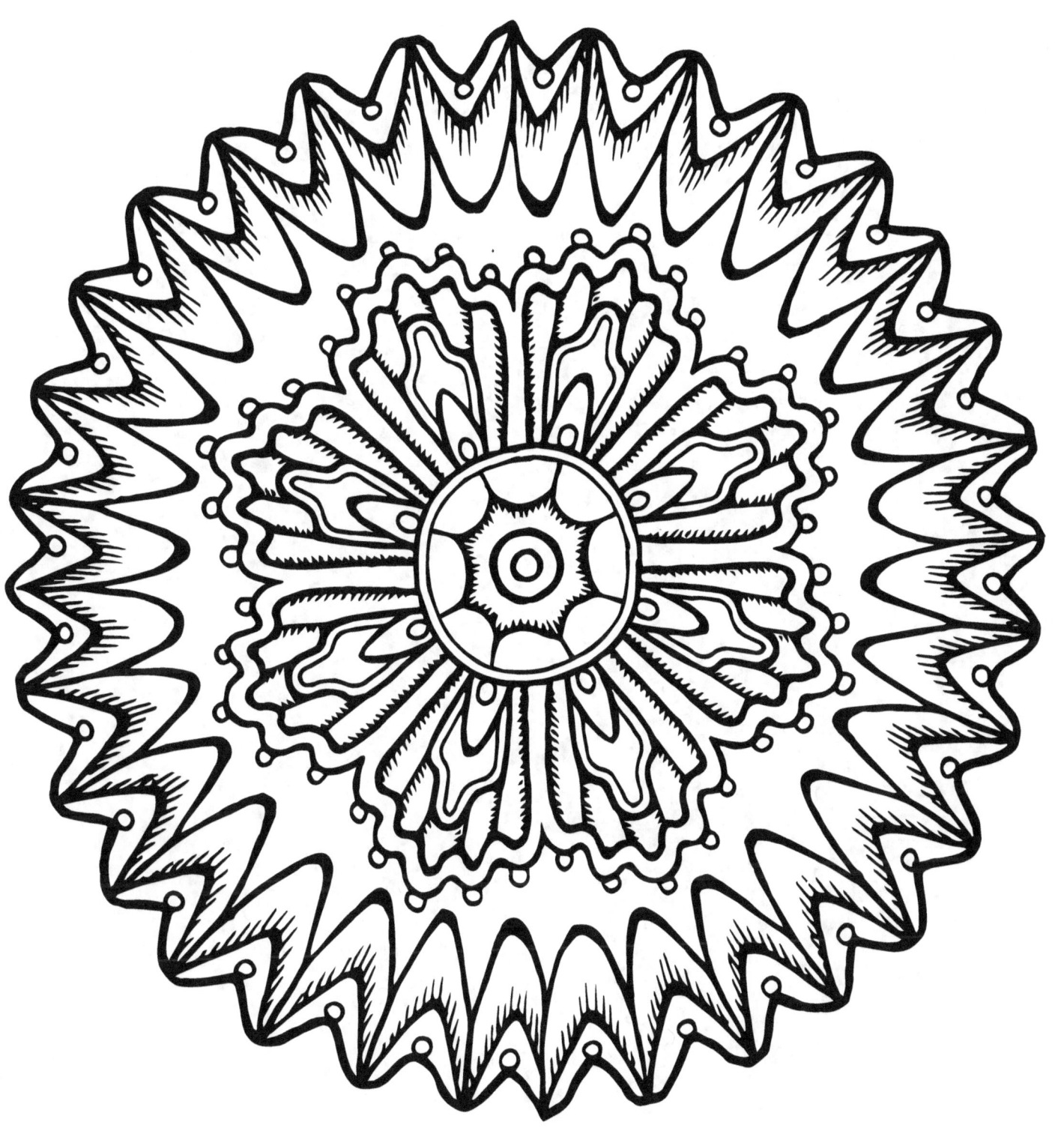

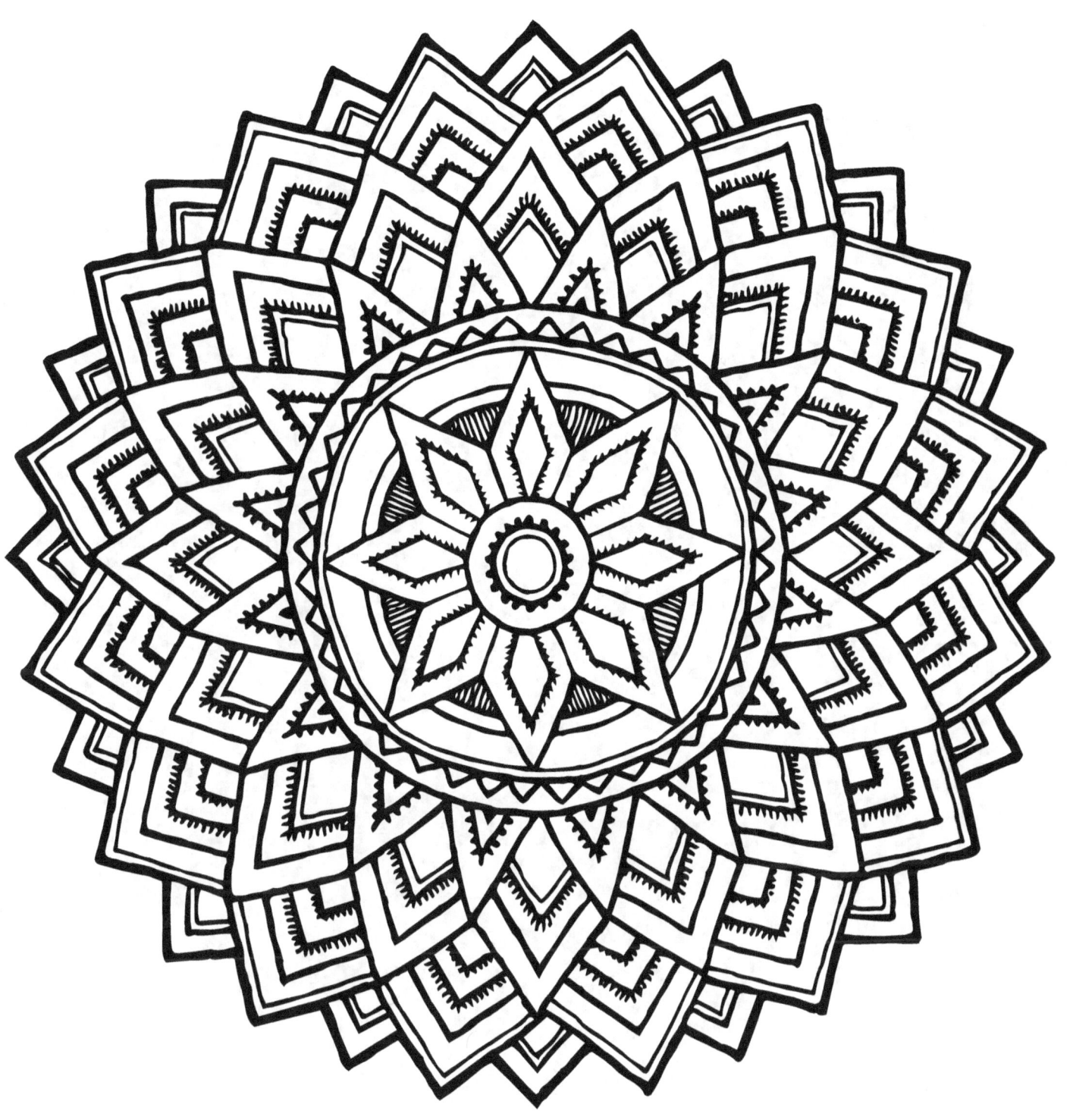

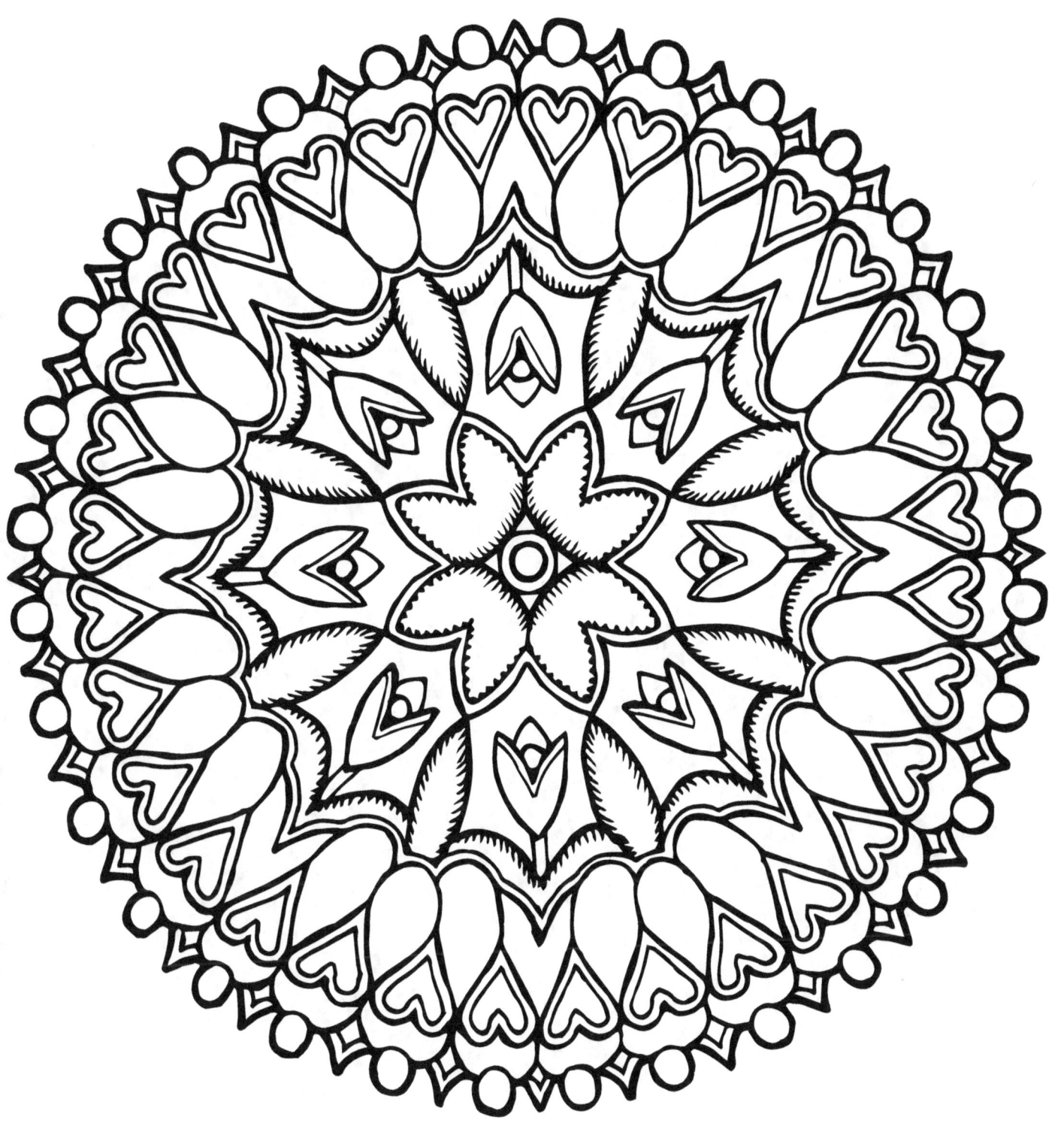

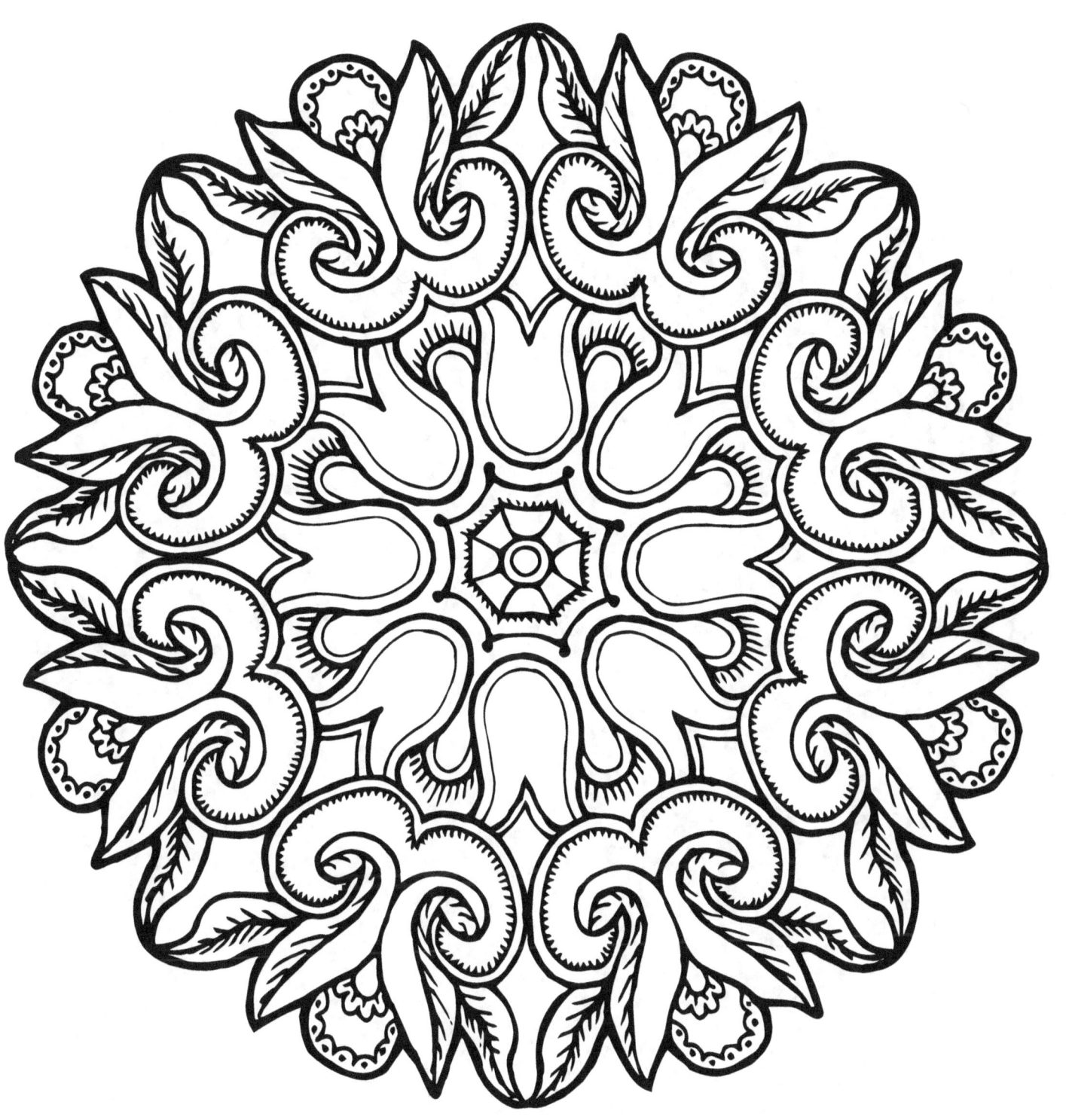

Books by Alberta Hutchinson

Home Made Books Coloring Books

Available from www.createspace.com (see specific web addresses below) and major booksellers:

MANDALA COLORING BOOK COLLECTION:

Mandala Designs Coloring Book No. 1 — 35 New Mandala Designs, (Revised in New Format)
   www.createspace.com/4506373

Mandala Designs Coloring Book No. 2 — 32 New Mandala Designs, (Revised in New Format)
   www.createspace.com/4555976

Mandala Designs Coloring Book No. 3 — 32 New Mandala Designs, (Revised in New Format)
   www.createspace.com/4614672

Mandalas Coloring Book No. 4 — 32 New Unframed Round Mandala Designs,
   www.createspace.com/5254882

Mandalas Coloring Book No. 5 — 32 New Mandala Designs, www.createspace.com/5298076

Mandalas Coloring Book No. 6 — 32 New Unframed Round Mandala Designs,
   www.createspace.com/5365617

Mandalas Coloring Book No. 7 — 32 New Unframed Round Mandala Designs,
   www.createspace.com/5385765

Mandalas Coloring Book No. 8 — 32 Intricate Round Mandala Designs, www.createspace.com/5479893

Mandalas Coloring Book No. 9 — 32 New Intricate Round Mandala Designs,
   www.createspace.com/5479893

MORE HUTCHINSON DESIGN COLORING BOOKS:

Fantasy Flowers Coloring Book No. 1 — 24 Designs in Elaborate Oval Frames,
   www.createspace.com/4446137

Fantasy Flowers Coloring Book No. 2 — 32 Designs in Elaborate Square Frames,
   www.createspace.com/4485357

Fantasy Flowers Coloring Book No. 3 — 32 Designs in Elaborate Oval-Rectangular Frames,
   www.createspace.com/5154200

Snowflake Designs Coloring Book — 24 Designs in Elaborate Frames, www.createspace.com/4446148

64 Christmas Ornaments Coloring Book, www.createspace.com/5186172

Make Your Own Book No. 1 — 50 Elaborate Round Frames for Coloring, with Text Lines,
   www.createspace.com/4704942

Make Your Own Book No. 2 — 50 Elaborate Oval Frames for Coloring, www.createspace.com/4765016

Mantra Meditation Coloring Book, www.createspace.com/5589496

Continued on the back...

OTHER COLORING BOOKS BY ALBERTA HUTCHINSON (available from major booksellers):

The Affirmations Colouring Book, by Louise Hay and Alberta Hutchinson, Hay House Publications
Mystical Mandala Coloring Book, Dover Publications
Infinite Coloring Mandala Design CD and Book, by Martha Bartfeld and Alberta Hutchinson, Dover Publications
Creative Haven Square Mandalas (Creative Haven Coloring Books), Dover Publications
Creative Haven Lotus Designs (Creative Haven Coloring Books), by Alberta Hutchinson, Dover Publications
3-D Coloring Book - Mandalas, by Martha Bartfeld and Alberta Hutchinson, Dover Publications

Other Books from the Home Made Books Collection

Available from www.createspace.com (see specific web addresses below) and major booksellers:

ILLUSTRATED POETRY AND MEDITATIONS:

Fireflies, by Rabindranath Tagore, illustrated by Alberta Hutchinson (color version),
www.createspace.com/5074812 (all proceeds donated to the Ninash Foundation)

Fireflies, by Rabindranath Tagore, illustrated by Alberta Hutchinson (black and white version),
www.createspace.com/5070674 (all proceeds donated to the Ninash Foundation)

Songs of Symmetry, poems and art by Alberta Hutchinson, in full color, www.createspace.com/4019375

Night Drawings and Meditations, meditations and framed art by Alberta Hutchinson, in full color,
www.createspace.com/5477788

My Palitana (India), story and art by Alberta Hutchinson, in full color, www.createspace.com/5423470

100 Meditations on the Sacred Healing Buddha, framed illustrations in full color by Alberta Hutchinson,
www.createspace.com/4938232, (all proceeds donated to Free Tibet)

CHILDREN'S PICTURE BOOK:

The Orphan and the Christmas Tree, by Edward C. Colwell, illustrated by Alberta Hutchinson,
www.createspace.com/3702633

NOVEL:

Step by Step, by Alberta Hutchinson, www.createspace.com/3669073